COMBAT HELICOPTERS

Yves DEBAY

HISTOIRE & COLLECTIONS

SUMMARY

From the TIGER to the APACHE, and from the CHINOOK to the PUMA "Combat Helicopters" presents in 295 photos the helicopters in service in the world. The particularly rich illustrations show these machines in action, from the arctic circle to the jungles of south America and from the steppes of Asia to the deserts of the Middle East.

The evolution, the history and the variations of 39 different models are studied in detail. The major airmobile units in the world and their tactical use are also presented ; from the new NATO airmobile division to the Paraguayan air force and from ALAT to the Japanese self defence force, the detailed battle orders of the world's helicopter forces have been carefully researched.

Current or potential hot-spots have not been forgotten and pictures taken in the field show helicopters of the Gulf and Balkan wars. The strengths of various forces, Indian, Pakistani, Greek or Turk for example are also given.

In 152 pages, "Combat Helicopters" will be a useful work of reference for the soldier, the diplomat, the spotter or the model maker.

OBSERVATION HELICOPTERS 8

ANTITANK HELICOPTERS 36

ASSAULT HELICOPTERS 72

HEAVY HELICOPTERS 120

INTRODUCTION

The genius Leonardo da Vinci made a drawing of one, and even though Professor Cierva's strange hybrid, the autogyro, had a limited success in the thirties, it was not until the second world war before the beginnings of a craft that was to revolutionise the world.

The first helicopters, developed by the Germans and the Americans at the end of that conflict were in fact nothing but unsightly piles of pipes, underpowered and despised by the pilots of the period. However the concept clearly had a future and flying without the need for long runways was soon to become a reality. Under the impetus of brilliant pioneers from Eastern Europe, Sikorsky and Piasecki, the USA launched the first really reliable machines, followed by France with the famous Alouette II which is still flying. The military very rapidly understood the advantages of such machines and they were used immediately for medical evacuations, resupplying and observation.

Relatively peaceful missions, until the day when the Americans, engaged in Korea, thought that the new machines could be used for transporting troops… some of these "flying lorries" were armed to protect themselves and thus the combat helicopter was born.

If the Korean war saw the first tactical use of the helicopter on a small scale then the Algerian war saw the birth of airmobility. Bigeard, Jean Pierre, Conan and others, by launching their paras to attack the Djebels through the air created a new type of combat; airmobile operations. This was the period of the Sikorski and the "bananas", skirting round, enveloping and cutting off the terrorised enemy. A new type of soldier was born, the helicopter commando, appearing suddenly from the sky, commanded from the sky and supported by fire from the sky. Ten years later in Vietnam, the Americans with their sense of excess, perfected the system and the 1st CAV became the first airmobile division in history, able to put more than four hundred machines into the air per operation. That war, lost more in the campuses than on the terrain itself, witnessed a surprising marriage; that of the helicopter and the missile which was to give rise to a very famous offspring. From then on, this new type of helicopter, essentially devoted to ground support was able to destroy tanks. The Russians even invented the Mi-24 flying tank (HIND its NATO code name) which filled thousands of Ethiopians, Angolans and Afghans with fear, before their efficiency was stopped by Stingers, sent by Reagan.

It was another monster, the AH-64 APACHE, which was amongst the first to fire several well-placed missiles on radar points in the Gulf war, creating a pathway for the F-117 stealth bomber… the revenge of the helicopter against the fixed wing.

Nowadays no armed force can do without the helicopter and any self-respecting country owes it to itself to possess a helicopter force. The frail "Licopters" of our grandparents day have now become impressive machines covered with missiles and crammed with electronics; but inside these engines of death, there is always a man who is willing to descend to refuel, resupply or look for the lost soldier through a hail of bullets. It is to these pilots that this book is dedicated.

Due to a lack of space, naval and SAR helicopters are not dealt with in this book. A second volume will fill that gap.

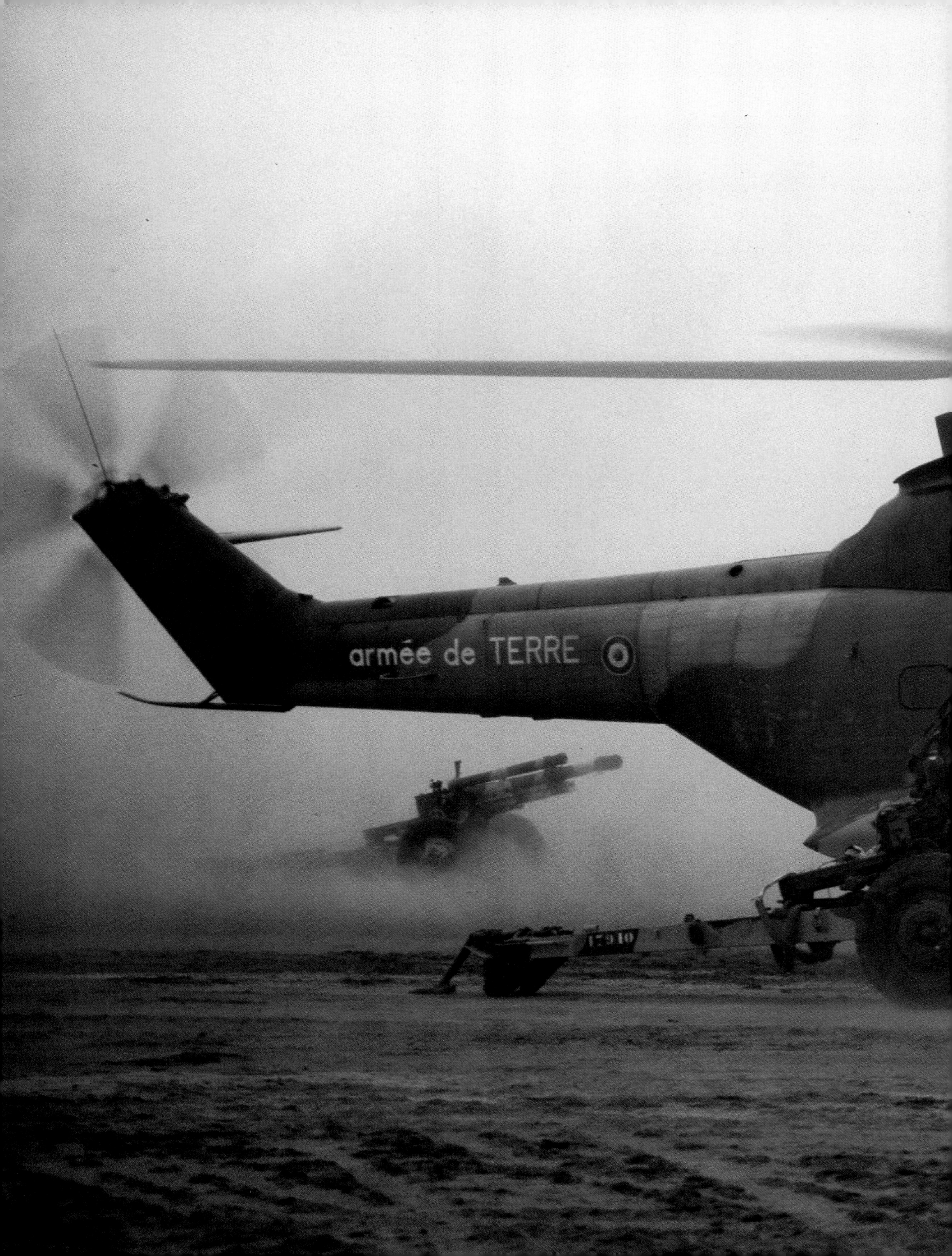
armée de TERRE

OBSERVATION HELICOPTERS

The first two missions attributed to rotating wing craft were those of observation and rapid liaison. The "flying bubbles", or Bell 47 and Alouette II revolutionised the chain of command and transmission; a General for example, after quickly boarding his helicopter, could inspect his units, take stock of a situation within a few minutes, and arrive unexpectedly to give his orders. The helicopter thus very quickly became a means of command but also a means of observation, unrivalled because of its lightness, flexibility and its ability to conceal itself behind cover and hills. It was able to fly at an altitude high enough to observe enemy lines or artillery fire. This was a long way from the restrictions of an observer in a hot air balloon or positioned in a bell tower. Because of its power of concealment, the helicopter replaced the vulnerable Piper Cub or Bird Dog. The war in Algeria saw a large scale use of the Alouette II and in the Vietnam war the flying egg OH-6A

Cayuse, called "Loach" by the GIs, was used. From then on complete units of light helicopters, bristling with rockets, were able to illuminate and find their targets. The 90's will see some of these helicopters armed, such as the OH-58 D or the Hugues 500, their agility making them an ideal tool for the US Special Forces which were to use these machines against armed Iranian oil rigs.

These days, things have scarcely changed, but the latest models have seen the trusty pair of binoculars replaced by a strange sphere above the rotor, or chin mounted under the nose. This magical sphere consists of TV sensors, an infrared image system and a laser rangefinder allowing observation and sometimes firing in all weathers and at night.

Apart from these missions, light helicopters remained the ideal thing for liaison, transport of senior staff and evacuation of medical personnel.

This Royal Army Air Corps Gazelle is seen with a light armoured scorpion of the 16 Lancer in the Tnönso Fjord.
This scene illustrates perfectly the cooperation that exists between helicopters and ground units.

*The OH-58 D and "Apache" duo will from now on form an integral part of the US Army. With its "ball" above the rotor,
the agile Kiowa will guide the "Apache" to its target. The machines shown here are from the aviation brigade of the 2nd armored division
used during operation REFORGER in Germany.*

ALOUETTE II
AEROSPATIALE SA-313B, SA-318C FRANCE

France achieved a worldwide success from the end of the 5O's with this first, mass-produced, light helicopter, as more than 1305 machines were built and adopted by 120 countries. Characterised by its bubble, its cockpit and its rear tubular structure, the Alouette II was the "Dragonfly" which was to make the public at large familiar with helicopters. The first prototype, built by the Societe National de constructions Aeronautiques du sud-est, renamed subsequently Aerospatiale, flew on 31 July 1952 with a Salmson 9NH piston engine. The Alouette was re-motorised several times, firstly with a Turbomeca 1 Artouste 1 for the SA-313 at the end of the 50's, then with the a more powerful Astazou turbine which gave rise to the definitive SA-318 version in 1964.

For a number of years the Alouette II performed many tasks, including observation and MEDEVAC and was even used as an armed helicopter. Nowadays, this machine can be considered historic, but remains in service in several armed forces, including in France where the last Alouette II in service is finishing its long career, which started in Algeria.

Opposite:
For three decades the Alouette II was the principal flying observation and liaison platform of the Bundeswehr. Several are still flying such as this one seen in Saxe during "CERTAIN SHIELD".

Before the appearance of the A-109, the Alouette II was the principal helicopter of the light aviation of the Belgian ground forces. Here an Alouette II takes off from Braschaal.

Characteristics

For the SA-318C
Alouette II Astazou.

L: 12.10m
Rotor diameter: 10.20m
Engines: one 530hp
Turbomeca Astazou IIA turbine.
Empty weight: 890 kg
With full load : 1650 kg
Maximum speed : 205 km/h
Cruising speed : 180 km/h
Autonomy : 720 km
Endurance : 5 h 18 min
for 580 litres of fuel.

An ALAT Alouette II is used here for observation and liaison, with the 1st Armoured Division at Mailly.

ALOUETTE III
SA-316, SA-319

The success of the Alouette II led the Aerospatiale Sud Aviation Company to develop a more powerful and more aerodynamic version. At the same time new equipment was adopted and the final result gave rise to an absolutely new machine, the SA-316A, which made its maiden flight in February 1959. The French Army acquired a large number of them and they were even used in Algeria, armed with SS-11 missiles which were very useful for firing into caves where the fellagas would hide. The Alouette III was thus, without doubt, the first helicopter to be armed with missiles. But it was principally within the Portuguese and Rhodesian armed forces involved in the tough bush war where the Alouette III was to prove its effectiveness. In Rhodesia, the G-CAR version was equipped with a twin Browning 30 and transported four infantrymen whereas the K-CAR was armed with a 20mm gun in the cabin. The South Africans took up this system in Angola. The Alouette III was licensed under the name of Chetak in the Indies, in Switzerland under its name of origin, and in Rumania under the code name IAR-316B. The Alouette III has disappeared progressively from the stocks of the ALAT, it remains in use in a number of armed forces and continues to be produced in a small number in the Indies.

Austria has 26 Alouette III. Here a machine from the Hubschnachergeschwader 2 of Aigenin Erstall.

The Dutch Alouette III attached to the 1st Army corps have long been flying over the plains of northern Germany, as seen here a machine of the 208th squadron at Soesterberg.

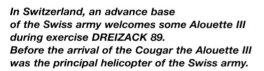

Rotor diameter: 11.02 m
Length: 12.84 m
Engine: one Turbomeca Astazou
XIV turbine developing 870hp
Empty weight: 1140 kg
Weight with full load: 2250 kg
Capacity: 575 l
Maximum speed: 220 km/h
Cruising speed: 197 km/h
Autonomy: 605 km with
six passengers.

A South African Alouette III flies over the Indian Ocean near the Cape. Apart from their intensive use in combat in Angola, the Alouette III of the SAAF carry out SAR and anti drug missions.

In Switzerland, an advance base of the Swiss army welcomes some Alouette III during exercise DREIZACK 89.
Before the arrival of the Cougar the Alouette III was the principal helicopter of the Swiss army.

THE NETHERLANDS
GROEP LICHTE VLIEGTUIGEN

As back-up for its army corps stationed in Germany, the Netherlands had a light air force set up attached to the army, the Groep Lichte Vleigtuigen, the headquarters of which were at Gilze-Rijen. The mission of the LV Group was and remains essentially liaison and observation flights from a stock of Alouette III and BO-105. An acrobatic patrol of an excellent standard, "the Grasshoppers", was formed in the seventies. The end of the Warsaw pact led the Dutch chiefs of staff to initiate a complete restructuring of its armed forces. A large number of armoured and mechanised units were disbanded, but in order to fulfil their NATO commitment, the Dutch committed themselves to creating a new airmobile brigade, the 11th Luchtmobiele Brigade which was to be at the disposal of the the Division Aeromobile Multinationale de l'Alliance. To support and transport the 11th Airmobile Brigade a large number of helicopters were ordered: 30 Apache, 13 Chinook and 17 Cougar. An amazing challenge therefore awaits the Gp LV pilots by the end of this century: to go from simple liaison missions to large and complex airmobile operations.

Stock: 62 Alouette III and 28 BO-105C. Apache, Chinook and Cougar are due to be delivered 1996-97.

Battle order:

208 squadron Soesterberg Alouette II
299 squadron Gilze-Rijen BO-105C
300 squadron Eindhoven Alouette III
will be equipped with Chinook in December 1995.
301 squadron Gilze-Rijen will be equipped with Cougar in 1996.
302 squadron Gilze-Rijen Alouette III.

In the "bubble" of his Alouette III a Dutch pilot consults his map.

The winter sunlight catches the fuselage of this BO-105 of the 299th squadron attached to the EM of the 13th armoured brigade for a firing exercise at Mourmelon. The colourwash on the roundel is a typical feature of the Dutch ALAT.

DENMARK

A Hughes 500 M waits for the order to take off with an RAF Chinook as part of exercise "BOLD GUARD" in 1990.

Some Fennec armed with the helitow missile system leave for a mission.
Note the striking two-tone camouflage, very effective on the plains of northern Europe.

A small country with an obvious strategic importance as it controls the Baltic straits, Denmark is considered by NATO as the door to the North sea.

The Danish army has a small aerial section, the Haerens Flyvetjaeneste or Royal Army Air Corps: made up of two companies, a reconnaissance equipped with Hughes 500M and an antitank company with Aerospatiale AS-550 C2 Fennec and Hughes 500M. The Fennecs are armed with the Swedish antitank system Helitow.

Stock: 12 Aérospatiale AS-550 Fennec and 12 Hughes 500M.

15

OH-6 CAYUSE MD-500 DEFENDER
MC DONNELL DOUGLAS HELICOPTER (HUGHES)

Born as a result of a request by the US Army for a light observation helicopter (LOH), the Hughes 369 model flew for the first time on February 27th 1963. 1434 models were adopted with the name 0H-6A Cayuse,

this veritable "flying egg" proved itself in Vietnam under the nickname "Loach". Sometimes armed with a Gatling mini-gun or an XM-75 40mm grenade launcher, the Cayuse was indissociable from all the other large helicopter operations of the conflict; nonetheless 658 models were lost in combat and 297 by accident. In 1968, the US Army relaunched the LOH programme and the Bell OH-58 was preferred to the OH-6D version retained by Japan. This choice sounded the death knell of the "Loach" in the US Army which withdrew its last models from service in 1992. Now outmatched, the OH-6A still flies in Bahrain (2), Brazil (4), Colombia (11), Dominican Republic (1), Honduras (4), Nicaragua (2), and Taiwan (6).

The success of the Cayuse led Hughes to develop a civil version, the Hughes 500, which was rapidly transformed into a military version for exportation and thus took the name of Model 500 M Defender.

Small but dangerous, an Israeli Hughes Defender leaves the Ramat David base for a night mission in South Lebanon.

Equipped with rocket pods one side and .50 machine gun pods on the other, this MD-520 of the 18 Tactical Air Support Philippin-Squadron is used in anti-guerilla operations.

Remotorised, this version was also built under license by Kawasaki of Japan as the OH-6J. It is not necessary to list all the modernised versions of the flying egg, but the version 0H-6D, equipped with a new rotor, is built under license in Argentina, Italy and Korea. It can be armed and therefore be used as a light attack helicopter, like the 500D Scout Defender equipped with cannon and rocket pods or the MD/TOW antitank. Some modified craft serve with the top secret US Army 106th Special Operations Aviation Regiment at Fort Campbell under the name of EH-6E, MH-6E and AH-6F. These machines would have played their part in the attack on Iranian oil rigs. The small size combined with the agility of the "Defender" was used a lot by the Israelis in night-time attack missions against the hesbollah in South Lebanon. The final development of the small Cayuse is the MD-530 Lifter equipped with a rotor with five blades and propelled by an Allison 250-C3 turbine developing 425cv. The 106th air force regiment of the special forces also uses the 530 under the nickname "Little Bird". Trials successfully attempted to use the "Little Bird" as a firing platform for snipers armed with 12.7mm precision guns. The revolutionary concept of NOTAR (No Tail Rotor) using a violent air current was also tested by the US Special Forces on MD 520/530 airframes.

Characteristics

For the model 500
Rotor diameter : 8.03 m - Length: 9.24 m
Engine : an Allison 250-C18A turboshaft developing 278 hp at take off.
Empty weight : 493 kg
Weight with full load : 1361 kg
Fuel capacity : 242 l
Maximum speed: 244 km/h
Cruising speed : 217 km/h
Mission radius : 606 km

A "flying egg" of the Argentinean army flies over the pampas.

AS-350 (AS-550)
ECUREUIL/FENNEC

The AS-350 Ecureuil, flown for the first time on 27th June 1974, was developed as a successor to the Alouette family as a multi-purpose four or five seater light helicopter. With the exception of civilian machines destined for the US market and propelled by a Textron Lycoming LTS 1O1, the standard version is equipped with a Turbomeca Arriel 1B. An armed version was developed as AS-350 L containing a great variety of military equipment, from the 20mm M-621, to 7.62mm machine gun pods as well as different varieties of rockets. At the request of Denmark, a light antitank helicopter version was studied carrying the Helitow missile system developed by Saab/Emerson. Twelve of these machines, capable of firing 4 Tow each, have been in service since 1991 in the Danish armed forces under the name AS-550 C2 Fennec.

Different versions of the Ecureuil are also constructed under license in Brazil by Helibras. Twenty Esquilo type armed helicopters make up the 1st battalion of aviation at Tabaube near Sao Paulo.

Characteristics

AS-550 Fennec	AS-555N Fennec
Rotor diameter : 10;69m	10.69 m
Length:12.94m	12.94 m
Engine: 1 Turbomeca	Two Turbomeca
Arriel 1D1	Arrius TM-3191M
developing 732hp	developing 456hp each for the
For the AS-550	AS-555
Weight: 1220 kg empty	1382 kg empty
Weight with full load: 2250 kg	2600 kg
Maximum speed: 287 km/h	278 km/h
Fuel capacity: 540 l	730 l
Mission radius: 666 km	722 km

The Danish Fennec equipped with the antitank Helitow system are a good compromise between firepower and lightness. 12 machines are in service and in one salvo a battalion of tanks can be destroyed.

This AS-555 of EHOM-68 is one of the "guardians" of Ariane. The craft is flying over the jungle of Guyana and the 20mm gun on the right is clearly seen.

AS-355 ECUREUIL 2
AS-555 FENNEC

A twin engine version of the AS-350 Ecureuil was developed in 1978 and the first of two prototypes flew on 28th September 1979. Many elements of the first, single engine version of the helicopter were conserved, the major changes being, of course, the propeller with two Turbomeca TM-319 Arrius, the transmission, the tanks and the structure of the fuselage. France is the main user of this version with a total of 52 machines.

The Fennec is used in the 67th squadron at Villacoublay. It ensures the transport of personnel and guards the Ariane rocket launch site with the EHOM 68 based in Guyana. For this task, the Fennec are used with a 20mm gun that is also found on 24 of the 44 AS-555 AN used as fighter helicopters by the Air Force. The ALAT also uses 10 AS-555 UN Fennec for night-flight training. Brazil also constructed the twin-turbine version and 13 HB-355 F2 Esquilo serve in the 1st squadron, 8th Aviation Group at Manaus as well as two machines within the Grupo de transporte Especial in Brasilia with two machines.

An HB-355 F2 Esquilo
of the Paraguayan air force being refuelled.
Note the light rocket launcher.

19

EUROCOPTER (MBB) BO-105

Dutch BO-105 of 309 squadron. These craft will serve as an observation platform for the Apache which enter service in 96.

It was on the 16th February 1967 that the BO-105 flew for the first time and was to reveal itself as one of the most agile helicopters of its generation, propelled in its standard B0-105C and B0-105CB version by two Allison turbines 250 C-20B.

The machine could carry five passengers as well as the pilot or six stretchers in the MEDEVAC version. The key to the agility of the BO-105, which can perform various acrobatics, lies in its titanium rigid rotor head.

The machine produced by Messerschmidt Bolkow at Donanworth is also assembled under license by CASA in Spain, IPTN in Indonesia and a civilian version by Eurocopter Canada. With 304 machines, the Bundeswehr is the main user of the B0-105 reconnaissance version with 100 BO-105M called VBH (Verbindungs und Beobachtungs Hubschrauber) and 212 BO-105 P antitanks (see page 52). The agile helicopter of the MBB had a certain success as an export item in all its versions and Iraq was the first importer with 75 machines followed by Spain which uses 70 BO-105. Indonesia built under license 130 NBO-105 with the exception of the rotors and the transmission which came from Germany. As a final point, Sweden has BO-105 used for observation and rescue under the name Hkp9B.

A FAMET BO-105 LOH in Andalucia during GALIA-88. The helicopter is built under license in Spain.

BO-105 CB of the Grupo of the Chilean air force flies over the lakes. Note the three aerials on the cockpit.

EUROCOPTER (MBB)
KAWASAKI BK-117

In fact, the BK-117 is not strictly speaking a military helicopter, but a machine developed simultaneously in Germany and Japan for civilian use. The first prototype flew in 1979. However some countries use it within their armed forces and indeed one craft, equipped with firing sights and eight HOT missiles, was presented at the 1985 Bourget air show.

From an output of 360 machines, only a small number is used by the military. 16 in Iraq used for SAR, 4 in Indonesia and 9 in South Africa which come from the old Bantustan (Ciskei, Transkei, Bophutatswana, Venda).

Characteristics

Rotor diameter: 11 m
Length: 13 m
Engines: Two Textron Lycoming LTS 101-750B
developing 708 hp at take off.
Empty weight: 1727 kg
Weight with full load: 3350 kg
Capacity: 697 litres plus 200 with auxiliary tank
Maximum speed: 278 km/h
Cruising speed: 250 km/h
Autonomy: 541 km

Recognisable by its three fins, a BK-117 from Bophutatswana flies over the "veld". Since the end of apartheid, the BK-117 of the old bantustans have formed a new squadron of the SAAF.

21

HEERESFLIEGER

The Heeresflieger or the aircraft of the German land army was born in the middle of the 50's along with the renaissance of the new German army. It was with American machines, typical of the period; Piasecki S-21 "Banane", S-58 "Choctaw" and "Sycamore", that the Heeresflieger made its first armies prior to the Alouette II. The sixties saw three types of machines begin their service which were to give the final character to light aircraft of the Bundeswehr; the Bell UH-1D and the CH-53 G built under US license, and the nationally constructed BO-105.

During the cold war, the potential enemy was only a few hours from the great industrial centres; the German military doctrine was reduced to its simplest form; do not give an inch of ground. The Heeresflieger was therefore conceived to bring maximum support to the panzers of the Bundeswehr with no real strategic objective since it would have been a question of fighting on their own ground. Each corps of the army (1st, 2nd and 3rd) had three helicopter regiments, an antitank of BO-105, one of medium transport on Bell UH-1D and one of "heavy" transport on

At the end of the cold war the BO-105 prowled close to the iron curtain.
The forests and woody hills give excellent cover in antitank combat.

Two BO-105 - PAH-1 of the 38th Panzerwehregiment move towards the waiting zone where they will go on to reach their objective.

CH-53 G. If the 105 operated directly on the front line with the panzerdivision, the transport units were conceived more for transporting Fallschirmjäger (parachutist) units of the Luftlande division by helicopter destined to "plug the holes" and lead an antitank counter-attack in case of enemy breakthrough. The transport units attached to an army corps could transport a battalion parachutist and his equipment into the combat zone by helicopter in two rotations. Each armoured or mechanised division also used a liaison staffel (flight unit) on Alouette II or B0-105 VBH and each army corps has a liaison and communication squadron.

An open-air briefing for these pilots of the Panzerwehregiment 16 where they are discussing the final points to an antitank mission.

23

HEERESFLIEGER

With the end of the cold war and the large budget reductions which followed, the Bundeswehr had to face, along with all NATO countries, an important restructuring and change of mission. With the creation of the NATO Rapid Reaction Force, and the Eurocorps, the Heeresflieger will, in future, be able to take on missions in territories on the periphery of the alliance. The structure of the army was modified as a consequence. Each corps kept the regiments of antitank helicopters but the means of transport were regrouped in the Heeresflieger Brigade 3 which transferred its machines to different units according to need. With the exception of the MI-8 unit, henceforth disbanded, no helicopter of the ex Volksarmee has been kept operational. Constantly modernised, Bell UH-1D and CH-53 G will stay as the transport linchpin beyond the year 2000, whereas the antitank machine crews are looking forward to having the PAH-2 Tiger which should begin service in the year 2000 under the name UHU. 75 UHU have been ordered and will ensure combat antitank missions, but a certain number of B0-105 P will remain in service. The NH-90 should replace the UHU-1D in the year 2002 but 124 modernised Iroquois will continue to fly in the Heeresflieger at the beginning of the 21st century.

Stock: 177 UH-1D, 52 BO-105 BSH (combat), 151 BO-105 PAH-1 (antitank). 96 BO-105 VBH (liaison and observation), 110 CH-53 G, 119 Alouette II.

After more than twenty years of good and loyal service, the CH-53 G is still the kingpin of German helicopter transport. The white belly of the machine indicates that it was used in Kurdistan for a humanitarian mission.

This view of 2 UH-1D Iroquois shows machines with the old camouflage and the new one which is two shades of green. These craft are taking part in exercise ALLEGRO EXCHANGE in North Italy.

Battle order:

The Heeresflieger Brigade 3 whose HQ is at Mendig is made up of three regiments of light transport with 48 Bell UH-1D each.
Heeresflieger regiment 6 at Jtzehoe.
Heeresflieger regiment 10 at Fassberg.
Heeresflieger regiment 30 at Niederstetten and three medium transport regiments with 23 BO-105 VBH and 36 CH-53 G each.
Heeresflieger regiment 15 at Rheine.
Heeresflieger regiment 25 at Laupheim.
Heeresflieger regiment 35 at Mending.

The three antitank regiments attached to each Army Corps and which use 60 BO-105 PAH-1, are the following:
Panzerwehr regiment 16 at Celle.
Panzerwehr regiment 26 at Roth.
Panzerwehr regiment 36 at Fritzlar.

Each army corps has its Stabstaffel on BO-105 VBH and their is also an independent unit of this type at Cottbus in ex East Germany. Each Panzerdivision or Panzergrenadier division has its liaison unit Heeresfliegerstaffel on Alouette II or BO-105 VBH. The Heeresfliegerstaffel bear the division number either: 1st, 4th, 5th, 7th, 10th, 13th, and 14th. As the Bundeswehr is in the middle of its expansion programme, unit numbers can be constantly modified.

The pilots of the Heeresflieger have the opportunity to fly in distant skies during NATO manoeuvres. Here a Bell UH-1D flies over a Turkish mosque.

GAZELLE SA-341/342

This well outlined small helicopter is the worthy successor of the Alouette II. It is a completely reconcieved helicopter, which made its first flight 12th April 1968. With its aerodynamic silhouette, technologically advanced rotor-heads, a redesigned cabin and above all, the revolutionary streamlined anti-couple rotor, called "Fenestron", the Gazelle SA-341 became a unique machine.

Great Britain showed an immediate interest and in 1967 the famous Anglo-French agreement concerning collaboration as regards helicopters was signed. Westland built the Gazelle and the Puma whereas the Lynx was adopted by the Marine Nationale. The first types of Gazelle SA-341 were propelled by a Astazou III turbine creating 590cv. Six versions were constructed initially: SA-341B for the British Army, SA-341C for the Royal Navy, SA-341D a training version for the RAF, HCC MK4 for VIP transport, SA-341H a military export version.

Westland closed its production lines in 1984 with 294 Gazelle built, 282 of those for the British Army. The Army Air Corps did not use the Gazelle armed, although certain machines were hastily equipped with rockets during the Falklands war. The principal missions of the British Gazelles remain liaison and observation, and for the latter task, 70 machines were equipped with AF-532 Ferranti magnifying glasses designed to locate targets. The ALAT received 170 SA-340F some of which were armed (see Armed Gazelles, page 50): 68 of these Gazelles were also equipped with SFIM M334 ATHOS target locating sights.

A more powerful version, the SA-342, flew the first time in May 1973, with a Astazou XIV turbine and was immediately adopted by the ALAT under the name SA-342 K, this model was relatively well marketed in the Arab world and adopted by the Iraqi, Syrian, Egyptian and United Arab Emirate forces. Egypt constructed 48 SA-342L's from 12 French "kits" under license and 12 models were equipped with a laser finding pod for SFIM Osloh 1 artillery.

Before the destruction of the SOKO factories at Mostar during the civil war, Yugoslavia built 132 SA 341-H Partizan under license and were to produce 170 SA-342L. The majority of these machines are in the hands of the Serbs.

Clearly recognisable by its tilted rotor named "Fenestron", the Gazelle is the principal combat tool of ALAT. Here a Gazelle of an observation squadron of the 5th RHC.

Above left:
The Gazelle was an export success and particularly in the Arab world where its lightness and ease of movement worked wonders. This is a Qatari model.

Above right:
Several metres above the ground a Gazelle of the Army Air Corps is heading towards 1st armoured division HQ During a NATO exercise in Germany. The Gazelle replaced the little Westland Scout in the British Army.

Characteristics

For the SA-341
Rotor diameter: 10.50 m
Length: 11.97 m
Engines: one Turbomeca
Astazou III turbine
developing 590 hp
Empty weight: 920 kg
Weight with full load: 1800 kg
Capacity: 445 litres
plus 290 l with
auxiliary tank.
Maximum speed: 310 km/h
Autonomy: 670 km

It is not exactly comforting to fly on a monoturbine for a long time over the sea. However, ALAT carries out maritime transfer once a year as part of exercise DAMTA. Here a machine of the 4th RHCM over the Mediterranean.

27

BELL MODEL 206-JET
AGUSTA BELL

In 1960 the US Army launched its LOH programme (Light Observation Helicopter) so as to have not only an excellent observation platform but also a machine capable of carrying out light transport, MEDEVAC and light support. The competition was won by the Hughes

An OH-58 B of the 3rd Staffel of the Austrian army landing during exercise WINTERSTURM 87.

OH-6 Cayuse but entrusting it with the qualities of its HO-4 model, Bell derived from it a 15-seat civilian version: the 206 model Jet Ranger which first flew in 1971. Some new modifications resulted in models 206B Jet Ranger II and III produced during the seventies. A large number of these civilian craft were militarised and used by a large number of armed forces. The 206 saw its last development with the more powerful 206 Long Ranger model which was ordered by Bangladesh, Cameroon, Guatemala, Mexico, Venezuela and the United States. Nonetheless it was the basic Jet Ranger which was to become the main liaison and observation helicopter of the US Army. In 1967 the Pentagon, thwarted by the increase in the cost and the delivery delays of the OH-6 Cayuse, relaunched the LOH competition, which was this time won by the Bell model 206 A. The fortunate winner received the military designation of OH-58A Kiowa, and from 1969 delivery of the 2200 models ordered by the US Army began. The model became also the principal light helicopter of the Canadian Armed forces under the name CH-139 with 88 craft in service.

Two OH-58 C Kiowa of the 2nd US Armoured division taking off from a clearing in Germany as part of REFORGER 89. The dark olive camouflage is particularly effective.

RANGER - BELL OH-58 A/B/C AB-206 JET RANGER

Australia constructed fifty-six Kiowa under license, known locally as Kalkadoon and Austria acquired 12 OH-58B in 1976. Moreover, from 1976 the US Army signed a contract with Bell to modernise its OH-58 A and to bring them up to the OH-58C standard by the addition of a new glass roof, a new Allison T-63 A720 420 cv turbine and the installation of systems to reduce the quantity of heat given out. A new control panel and modernised avionics were also integrated in this version. 435 OH-58A were thus reconverted into OH-58C from 1978. Israel Aircraft Industries modified a new section of 150 craft destined for the US forces in Germany in 1985. The Italian firm Agusta also built the Bell 206 under license and of 7000 Jet Rangers produced a good 1000 of these were made in Italy and a large number of these craft were exported.

Characteristics

Rotor diameter: 10.16 m
Length: 11.94 m
Engines: one Allison 250-C2
turbine developing 317 hp
Empty weight: 682 kg
Weight with full load:
Fuel capacity: 288 l
internal with
extra tank 544 l
Maximum speed: 226 km/h
Cruising speed: 214 km/h
Mission radius: 673 km

In the beautiful Dolomite region a small AB-206 attached to the Alpini Corps has just landed as part of a liaison mission.

29

OH-58 D KIOWA WARRIOR

With its "ball" above the rotor, the OH-58D has a comical appearance but this machine is without doubt the "*nec plus ultra*" as far as observation helicopters are concerned. It proved itself during the Gulf War. It was in September 1981 that the model Bell 406 was selected to be the springboard of the AHIP programme (Army Helicopter Improvement Programme), with the idea of developing a reconnaissance helicopter capable of carrying out not only observation missions and to regulate artillery fire, but also to act as a support for assault helicopters. Five prototypes were built and the first flight took place on 6th October 1983. It was followed by a test programme operational on the top-secret bases of Yuma and Edwards which were completed with success in February 1985. 315 machines were ordered in 1985 and a second batch of 12 OH-58D were also ordered so as to replace those helicopters lost during the Gulf war. The OH-58D began its service within observation squadrons of the US Army in 1985, and from September 1987 several machines were armed with Hellfire and Stinger missiles, rocket pods and 12.7mm machine guns within the framework of operation "Prime Chance", designed to fight against the Iranian rapid launches. This success led the US Army to modify some 315 OH-58D in service into KIOWA Warrior 243. The OH-58D is distinguishable from the OH-58C by its spherical observation mast, and its four blade rotor in composite material. The "ball", or "mast mounted sight", is the "raison d'etre" of the OH-58D. It comprises two windows used for the optics of a battlefield surveillance camera and an infrared scanner twinned with a laser rangefinder, which permitted the search for navigational targets whatever the weather conditions. The OH-58D is from this point on indissociable from the AH-64 Apache whose very effective successor it was. 81 craft are to be modified into MPLH (Multi Purpose Light Helicopter) so as to serve in the US rapid reaction force, and Bell is studying a new version which will be equipped with new avionics, colour digital maps and a GPS. The pilot and observer will be equipped with a special helmet linked to the observation mast.

With the exception of Taiwan, which ordered 12 craft plus 14 on option, the OH-58D is only in service in the US Army.

Opposite: At an airport near the Rhine, a squadron of OH-58 D of the 4th Aviation regiment of the 8th Infantry division wait for permission to take off. The unit has now been disbanded but its advanced material will be kept.

Two OH-58 D of the 1/17 Cav attached to the famous 82nd airborne division train in difficult terrain, here flying over the desert.
Helicopters of this type will guide not only Apache but also British Lynx and Gazelle HOT of ALAT.

Characteristics

Rotor diameter: 10.67 m
Length: 12.85 m
Engine: One Allison T 703 AD-700 turbine developing 650 hp
Empty weight: 1381 kg
Weight with full load: 2041 kg
Fuel capacity: 341 kg
Maximum speed: 241 km/h
Cruising speed: 204 km/h
Autonomy: 463 km
Endurance: 2 h 24 min.

AGUSTA A-109

Agusta, one of the oldest Italian aeronautic firms, specialised in the construction, under license, of American Bell helicopters during the fifties which created a solid export success. However, in 1967, the transalpine company began the construction of its own model, the Agusta A-109, three prototypes of which were built, the first flying on 4th August 1970. Production started with a slight delay and from 1976, machines named A-109C Hirundo, able to transport 8 passengers, were constructed, essentially for the civilian market. Some Hirundo were bought by the military, including several by Argentina. Two of the four craft used by the Argentineans were captured intact by the British during the Falklands war and reused by the 7th regiment of the Army Air Corps. As the Agusta A-109 was seen to have a certain military potential, the esercito modified 24 of them under the name A-109 EOA (Elicottero d'Osservazione Avanzata) propelled by two Allison 250-C2 OR turbines. The first machines of this type were delivered in 1988 and are distinguishable by their large doors, SFIM M-334-25 sight also equipped with a laser rangefinder mounted on the cabin, as well as self-filling tanks and electronic counter-measure equipment. Belgium was also interested by this slightly modified model which, under the name A-109 BA started service within the aviation wing of the land forces with 18 reconnaissance and 24 antitank versions. These craft were manufactured under license by SABCA. With 15 examples of a new A 109 K version sold to Swiss mountain rescue units. Agusta hoped to make a breakthrough on the export market.

Characteristics

Rotor diameter: 11 m
Length: 13.5 m
Engines: 2 turbomeca Allison 250-C2 OR developing 700 hp each at take off.
Empty weight: 1595 kg
Weight with full load : 2850 kg
Capacity: 700 l
Maximum speed: 266 km/h - Cruising speed: 259 km/h
Mission radius: 537 km

An Italian Agusta A-109 of the esercito takes off from Viterbo, the large training base of Italian light aviation. The craft is a type used for experimenting with various equipment as the observation sight above the cockpit proves.

First operational sortie for these Agusta-109 Tow of the Belgian 18th antitank Bn during COLD GROUSE 95 in Denmark.

BELGIUM
LAND FORCES LIGHT AVIATION
LICHTVLIEGWEZEN VAN HET LANDMACHT

From the end of the fifties, the small light aviation of the Belgian land forces acquired a very high level and was considered amongst the best in NATO. For thirty years, Belgian pilots in their Alouette II carried out, for the 1st corps in Germany, liaison and observation missions. One of their great specialities was tactical flying, skimming over the ground in the German forests. With the recent appearance of antitank helicopters, light aviation has to adapt to new missions and the 18th battalion are striving for the success of the new NATO airmobile division. Apart from the service units, the Belgian antitank helicopter battalions are comprised of two antitank companies (2 HO and 7 HA) and one observation section (5 HO). The stock consists of 28 Agusta A-109 HA each one equipped with 8 Helitow, 18 Agusta A-109 HO observation and 20 Alouette II.

Some Alouette II taken near Cologne at the time when the Belgian 1st corps were in Germany in 1985.

The organigram is as follows:
16th liaison battalion Alouette II.
17th antitank battalion A-109HA and A-109HO.
18th antitank battalion A-109HA and A-109HO.
The three units are based at Bierset near Liege.

An A-109 of the 18th Bn in its observation version.

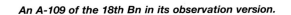

33

SIKORSKY S-76/H-76 EAGLE

Amongst very "Pacific war" surroundings,
this Philippino S-76 leaves for an anti-guerilla mission.

Basically, the S-76 is a civilian bi-turbine machine developed by Sikorsky for transporting 8 to 12 passengers and propelled by two Allison 250-C30 650cv turbines. It flew for the first time on 13th March 1977. It was followed by an improved version, the S-76 Mark II and a simpler version, the S-76 Utility. This became of interest to the military and was rapidly transformed into AUH-76; a combat version with sliding doors, optional armour, defence avionics and a whole range of weaponry ranging from rocket pods to a gun or an antitank missile. The engine comprised two Pratt and Whitney PT-6B-36 A 981cv turbines and was known by the name S-76 B. Spain ordered the same airframe, but with Turbomeca Ariel 1S1, 732cv turbines under the name S-76C. A highly militarised version derived from the AUH-76, the H-76 was offered for export. With the exception of the Philippines which used it in combat against rebel communist and Islamist movements, the S-76 was mainly used for VIP transport or at the end of training.

Characteristics

Rotor diameter: 13.41 m
Turning rotor length: 16 m
Length of fuselage: 13.22 m
Engines: two Pratt & Whitney
Canada PT-6B-36
developing 960 hp
Empty weight: 2545 kg
Weight with full load: 5171 kg
Internal capacity: 993 l
Maximum speed: 287 km/h
Cruising speed: 269 km/h
Autonomy: 578 km

An S-76 of the Philippines flying over the beautiful south sea beaches, on the look out for guerrillas. Note the FN Herstal machine gun pod.

EUROCOPTER AS-365 PANTHER

A Pantera HM-1 of the 1st Batalhào de Helicopteros at its Brazilian base. Brazil is the main military user of the Pantera.

Conceived basically as a civilian monoturbine helicopter, the AS-361 H was developed and gave rise to the AS-365 M Dauphin. This military version is capable of being used as a light assault helicopter with a dozen men on board or antitanks with eight HOT missiles or 44 SNEB missiles. The improved AS-365 K prototype was given the name PANTHER and gave rise to several versions, AS-565 AA armed, AS-565 CA antitank, AS-565 UA troop transport and AS-565 UA and SA, these latest naval versions have had a great export success. The ground version was retained by Brazil where the HELIBRAS company acquired the license and built 36 craft which, since then, have become the "Jack of all trades" of the Brazilian army under the name HM-1 "PANTERA". The other large user of the Panther is Angola with 16 machines, 6 of which are AS-565 armed with a 20mm gun.

China constructed the naval version under the name of Haitun Z-9 and it is not impossible that a land version was based on it.

Characteristics

Rotor diameter: 11.94 m
Turning rotor length: 13.68 m
Length of fuselage: 12.11 m
Engines: Two Turbomeca Arriel turbines each developing 749 hp
Empty weight: 2193 kg
Weight with full load: 4250 kg
Fuel capacity: 1135 l with internal tank + 180 l
Maximum speed: 296 km/h
Cruising speed: 278 km/h

A mission on the amazonian "Selva" for this Pantera. Often the helicopter is the sole means of getting supplies to commandos cut off in the jungle.

ATTACK HELICOPTERS

From its conception, the helicopter was armed as the very little known Fa-223 Luftwaffe transport which were equipped with an MG-15 in their glass nose for self-defence. It was during the Korean war, when rotating wing craft were in their infancy, that machines were armed, as the H-19 "Chickasaw" (Sikorsky S-55) equipped with rockets or such as the small Bell 47's equipped with a Bazooka. That was a matter of improvisation depending on the situation on the battlefield. No doctrine as such was established. At the height of the cold war the influence of the Pentagon moved more towards ballistic missiles or strategic bombers rather than to this new highly tactical and rather scorned weapon.

At the time the helicopter remained a "gadget" for Generals or as possibly a means of transport. The French army, confronted with the harsh reality of events in Algeria knew how to make the best of the technical quality, though still mediocre, of the helicopters and to draw up a real doctrine of use; some machines were armed with 20mm guns, rockets and even SS-10 and SS-11 missiles conceived basically as antitank but proved themselves invaluable in anti-guerilla combat. The French example was to lead the US General Vanderpool, pioneer of American aeromobility, to create the experimental aerial combat and reconnaissance unit considered as "laughable" by a large number of senior figures in the US army. It was not before 1962 that a unit was formed at Okinawa and sent to Vietnam where it showed itself to be very versatile that the critics changed their mind. Two years later, the 1st CAV, 1st division of airmobile cavalry, entered into history with a great deal of success. Nonetheless, a real"aerial cruiser" designed for troop support, was still lacking. Before this shake-up, all armed helicopters were modified versions of standard machines, such as Huey, equipped with rockets and miniguns which supported assault landings of the CAv at Drang (Vietnam).

The solution came with the two-seater AH-1 Cobra, both armoured and armed with guided missiles which, from 1967, were used in service. The "snake" damaged the N.Vietnamese PT-76 and T-55 by destroying the TOW antitank missiles. A brilliant career which continues to this day.

In the west, in order to counter the massive quantity of the 50,000 combat tanks of the Warsaw pact, the French, Germans and British, rather than developing costly combat helicopters, preferred to arm existing Gazelle, Lynx and BO-105 with missiles, and to develop tactics centred on large scale mobility. In the seventies, a thunderbolt shook the west with the appearance of a real Soviet flying tank, the MIL Mi-24 Hind. This helicopter, practically invulnerable to light calibre was the backbone of the large Russian expansion in Angola, Ethiopia and Nicaragua and indeed was intensively by the Red Army in Afghanistan. only the release of Stinger missiles by the Americans on the Angolan and Afghan guerrillas stopped the "Red Monster". With the Apache, the future Tiger, the Mangusta, the Rooivalket and the later Kamovs, the attack helicopter, laden with electronic devices and rockets and missiles, has once and for all gained its place on the modern battlefield. It was the AH-64 Apaches which "started the ball rolling" during the Gulf war, paving the way for the furtive aeroplanes (such as the F-117 "Stealth") by destroying radar cover... A surprising fate for a craft with unremarkable origins.

Above: Blending into the background at Verdon, a squadron of armed Gazelle of the 3rd RHC approach a firing position.

Opposite: An extremely advanced machine, the Apache is without doubt the most effective combat helicopter currently in service. Here, armed with 12 Hellfire missiles, an Apache of the 1/3 bat. of the 2nd US Armoured division is hovering in a Bavarian forest.

Vs HELICOPTERS

During the Algerian war, type S-55 or Piasecki helicopters were armed with 20mm guns, side firing and nicknamed "Pirate". These helicopters relied on assault landings to clear landing zones of all enemy presence. It was of course, out of the question to shoot down other helicopters when the rebels did not possess any. On its return to France, ALAT abandoned the 20mm guns in order to develop helicopters equipped with antitank missiles so as to counterbalance the formidable superiority in tank missiles of the Warsaw pact; the threat coming from possible Soviet combat helicopters was judged to be negligible.

The Kippour war in October 1973 however changed this frame of mind as Egyptians and Syrians had led several effective aeromobile operations with their Mi-8 of Soviet manufacture. It was doubtless during one of these operations over the Sinai where the first combat between helicopters took place. Flying parallel to an Egyptian Mi-8 an Israeli Super Frelon shot it down by means of a machine gun fired through a wide open side door. This war showed that the Russians and their allies were capable of using their component aeromobile on a large scale. The putting into service of the Mi-24, several years later, only served to accentuate this observation. Fleets of helicopters risked confrontation near the battlefield. The French thought once again of the 20mm gun and equipped their RHC (Regiments of Combat Helicopters) with a squadron of Gazelle/gun, with the responsibility of engaging their pursuers. The Spanish also installed a Rheinmetall gun on their B0-105. Some of these helicopters were used very efficiently by the Iraqis who sank a number of small Iranian boats in the Fao marshes. It was also during this war that the first "dog fight" took place when an Iranian Cobra shot down

A Gazelle of the 3rd RHC opens fire on a ground target. Note the ejection of the cartridges.

In the Andalucian dust, two BO-105 gunships of the FAMET take off for an attack mission as part of exercise GALIA 88 near Cordoue. Note the streamlined ammunition belt of the 20 mm gun.

an unarmed Iraqi Gazelle. Nowadays many helicopters can be equipped with a gun pod as much for light ground attack as for a duel with another machine. The next step was of course the adoption of air to air missiles by helicopters and because of this were able, in ideal firing conditions, to shoot down a jet. The Stinger, Sidewinder and Mistral missiles equipped, however, helicopters for attack or for their own defence.

During the gulf war the 1st RHC experimented with the CELTIC system consisting of a Mistral missile mounted on a Gazelle equipped with a brief firing system. This perfected system seen here at Al Rafah gave rise to the Gazelle Mistral which is beginning to equip ALAT.

AH-1 F/S COBRA

It would need a complete book to describe in detail the history and development of the AH-1 Cobra, first attack helicopter and 1100 examples of which were produced for the US Army. With its distinctive narrow fuselage, the Cobra rapidly became legendary. In order to use it the US Army had to practically fight with the USAF who wanted the monopoly on tactical combat machines. This craft made the rotor enter a new phase of its history: pure combat. Two-seater, capable of counter-attacking with its mini-gun and rockets, the Cobra was an assault craft conceived to clear the landing zone and open the way for the squadrons of Huey 3. From the Autumn of 1967, the Cobra in its G version was engaged in Vietnam and, despite certain losses, made a contribution in breaking the Vietcong offensive of Easter 1972.

The follow-up to the history of the Cobra consists of a series of modifications which ceaselessly improved the performance of the basic model. The Q model was the first to be equipped with eight TOW missiles but this model proved to be under-motorised and gave rise to, after modernisation, the AH-1 S series which is the current standard type of the US army as well as the model AH-1F generally destined for exportation. With the exception of the flat glass roof, the basic structure has not in fact been changed and the S model still has this fine reptile-like silhouette. The nose and the cockpit have, of course, been modified in order to carry the TOW aiming system. The Cobra pilots were the first to use a helmet linked to the chin turret, allowing the three tube 20mm M-197 guns to follow the movements of their head. The principal weapon is constituted of eight TOW missiles carried on two pylons on each side of the craft.

A great number of rocket-launcher pods can be carried and complete the action of the 20mm gun. Certain craft have been equipped with thermal image and passive protection systems. The AH-1S remains, in general, the helicopter of aerial cavalry units and therefore protects reconnaissance machines whilst waiting for the engagement of the Apaches. The Cobra has also seen some action, with Tashal in the Lebanon and one of them carried out a spectacular rescue operation by bringing back a jet pilot, from Lebanon to Israel, hanging from its undercarriage.

Opposite: This unique silhouette haunts the skies of all five continents. Like the Dakota, the Cobra will remain an historic machine in service beyond the year 2000. Here a machine of the 2nd Armoured Cavalry Regiment during REFORGER 89.

Not far from the Czech border, an AH-1S Cobra and its "Loach" observe the advance of tanks of the 2nd Armoured Cavalry Regiment. These helicopters are part of that elite unit which keep the traditions of the cavalry of the Indian wars.

Characteristics

Rotor diameter: 13.41 m
Length: 16.18 m
Height: 4.09 m
Engines: one Textron Lycoming
T-53 turbine
developing 1290 hp
Empty weight: 2993 kg
Weight during combat: 4524 kg
Capacity: 980 l
Maximum speed: 315 km/h
Cruising speed: 227 km/h
Mission radius: 507 km

41

At Palmahim base south of Tel Aviv an Israeli AH-1F from 191 squadron awaits its pilot for a mission.
Note the sand colouring and the large yellow V markings of the Tsahal. Israeli Cobra are intensively used in south Lebanon.

A formation of Pakistani AH-1F with their OH-58 C for observation. The F model, very similar to the S, is reserved for export.

AH-1W SUPER COBRA

The AH-IJ and AH-IT, Whisky version, the principal attack helicopter of the famous Marine corps and derived from bi-turbine models, can be considered the most powerful of the Cobras hence the name; Super Cobra. The craft is longer and has a chin turret and fin different from previous models. It is because of these large "gills" that the W model is instantly recognisable. These large spouts are for the exhaust of the two T-700-GE-401 turbines giving rise to 1690 cv and means that, with its cruising speed of 282 km/h, the Super Cobra has one of the best weight/power ratios of any attack helicopter in service. The avionics and the armaments have, of course, been considerably modernised, and, during the Gulf war, the Super Cobra of the USMC destroyed 60 tanks in one mission. The Super Cobra fired the complete range of American missiles and can even use simultaneously antitank TOW and Hellfire and air to air AIM-9L. Four to nineteen round LAU-61A, LAU-86A, LAU-68 rocket pods with Hydra 70 projectiles could equally be used. Foreign users include Turkey which has already engaged its ten Super Cobra in Kurdistan and Thailand with 18 models plus 24 as an option. Under the name of Cobra Venom the AH-1W and its weapon system was proposed to Great Britain for its acquisition programme for a new attack helicopter. This proposition was refused as, at the last moment, the British chose the Apache.

(1) The USMC machines considered as "naval helicopters" are not dealt with in this volume.

The Turkish Super Cobra have a very effective combat camouflage. The craft armed with two rocket pods LAU-68 belongs to the school at Güvercinlik near Ankara which is often engaged in Kurdistan.

WESTLAND LYNX

A product of the famous Anglo-French helicopter programme of February 1967, the Westland Lynx is truly a multi-purpose machine. Even though the project was studied entirely by Westland, 30% of mechanical parts making up the Lynx were manufactured by Eurocopter France (notably the four blade titanium rotor heads). All versions of the Lynx use a digital control system which, added to an "all weather" avionic, was the first helicopter of this model designed to operate in extreme weather conditions. The first prototype, followed by six others, flew 21st March 1971. The MK-1 version was designed to become the combat helicopter of the British army and started its service in Autumn 1971. Since then, this craft has earned itself a justifiable reputation for robustness and multi-purpose use. Apart from antitank missions the Lynx can carry twelve soldiers as well as its two-man crew. In its antitank version the Lynx carried eight TOW missiles directed by means of a stabilised sight situated on the left of the cockpit roof.

113 Lynx AH-MK 1 were constructed for the Army Air corps and the Royal Marines. Almost all these machines were modified to MK-7 standard with an improved rear rotor, a new avionic, and large hot air shafts in the shape of a cube. The Lynx did not participate in the Falklands, however 23 Lynx from 654, 659 and 661 squadrons took part in combat in the Gulf. Several minutes before the cease-fire of 29 February 1991 a craft from 659 squadron destroyed a GAZ 69 Jeep, thus firing the last missile of the war. The last version of the Lynx which began service in 1991 was the AH-MK-9, immediately recognisable by its long flat nose and its three-wheeled undercarriage. The craft kept its MK-7 modifications but uses improved navigation instruments. The MK-9 can also carry more weight and an extra tank can also be installed.

In its land based military version the Lynx was not exported, but 150 models, including 26 MK-9 serve with the British armed forces.

Easily recognisable by its wheels, a Lynx Mk-9, latest version of the machine, leaves Ploce to fly over Bosnia.
The craft belongs to 663 squadron of the 3rd regiment of the Army Air Corps. As opposed to the MK-7 destined the MK-9 is for light troop transport.

Version MK-7
Rotor diameter: 12.80 m
Length: 15.63 m
Height: 3.66 m
Engines: Two Rolls Royce GEM-41-1
turbines developing 1120 hp each.
In 1987 the turbines were brought up to
GEM-42 standard developing 1135 hp
Empty weight: 2578 kg
Weight with full load: 4876 kg
Fuel capacity: 973 l plus
two variations of extra tanks
in the fuselage with 214 l
and 873 l capacity respectively.
Maximum speed: 259 km/h
Cruising speed: 130 km/h
Autonomy: 634 km
With reserve tanks: 1342 km.

An MK-7 Lynx of the British army of the Rhine flies over a lake near Hanover.

45

ARMY AIR CORPS

Compared with France and the U.S., Great Britain became interested in aeromobility rather late. This was probably due to the fact that at the end of the 50's (the beginning of aeromobility), the British were involved in maintenance of order operations in the Malaysian jungle or in an urban environment as in Cyprus or Aden. Terrain which did not need large aeromobile formations.

However, the Whirlwind, Bristol, Belvedere and other Dragonfly were extremely useful during this period. It was that which gave rise to the helicopter force of HM Forces. Currently, the Army Air Corps and the RAF shared engaged helicopters for land operations.

Whether it was with NATO forces, in Germany, the Gulf, the Falklands or in Northern Ireland, the Army Air Corps has always known how to maintain, in the serious way for which it is renowned, the great British military traditions. The origin of the corps is found in the small Auster or Piper aeroplanes which adjusted artillery fire at the end of the second world war. Nowadays, with the little Westland Scout having been abandoned, the Army Air Corps only uses two types of machines, the Lynx and the Gazelle, forming the heart of the 1st, 3rd, 4th, 5th and 9th Army Aviation Regiment. The 1st and 9th regiments operate respectively in aid of the 1st Armoured Division in Germany and the 3rd (UK) division and its units, with an antitank role, each one composed of three squadrons of 6 Lynx MK-7 and 6 Gazelle, making a total of 36 helicopters. The 3rd and 4th regiments are implemented with the famous 24th aeromobile brigade. As in other regiments, the first two squadrons flew with 6 Lynx MK-7 and 6 Gazelle, but the third squadron is reinforced and is comprised of 12 Gazelle, 12 Lynx MK-7 and 12 Lynx MK-9. The latter are used mainly to bring infantry troops on the terrain and are armed with ATK Milan or AA Javelin missiles. The 5th regiment operates in Northern Ireland and there are small "flights" of independent Gazelles. The former squadron of the 3rd brigade commando which used to fly with Royal Marine craft was attached recently to the Army Air Corps.

A Gazelle AHMK-1 attached to the AMF (Allied Mobile Force) for the duration of exercise ANCHOR EXPRESS 86 flies in North Norway.

A war-like atmosphere on the terrain near Ploce where some Lynx attached to the UN rapid reaction force are getting ready. A Lynx MK-7 hovers above a row of Lynx MK-9 of the 3rd regiment.

Lastly, let us mention the presence of the Flight No. 8 with 4 A-109 (two of which were captured from the Argentineans) and are used by the highly secretive SAS. The order of 67 Apache Longbow WAD-64D delivered in 1987 made the Army Air Corps enter a new era and modified the structure of this section. The Apache began service in combat helicopter units and are attached to the 24th aeromobile brigade and to two armoured divisions, with two squadrons of 16 craft and two other squadrons reduced to 6 machines. The 20 remaining will be kept in reserve.

Maintenance during combat as part of CERTAIN SHIELD in Germany.
An armourer checks the electronic system of the TOW while a mechanic inspects the rotor head.

Stock: 4 Agusta A-109, 160 Gazelle AH Mk1, 110 Westland Lynx AH MK-7, 26 Westland Lynx AH MK 9, 67 AH-64 D Apache on order.

Battle order:

On Lynx Mk-7 and Gazelle: sqn 651, sqn 652, sqn 654, sqn 655, sqn 656, sqn 657, sqn 661, sqn 662, sqn 663, sqn 665, sqn 669, sqn 672, sqn 673.
On Lynx Mk-9: sqn 653 and sqn 659.
On Gazelle: sqn 658, sqn 666, sqn 670, sqn 671, and Flight N°2, N°3, N°6, N°7, N°12, N°16, N°29.
On A-109: Flight N°8.
The training squadron 667 and the 3rd Commando Brigade Air squadron operate with Gazelle and Lynx MK-7.

At the time when the Red Army was still a threat, British pilots trained to "break the tank". Here in the Weser valley Lynx attached to the 1st Armoured division establish a forward base.

THE ROYAL AIR FORCE

The prestigious Royal Air Force has, of course, gained an incomparable experience in the use of its helicopters over the years, as much in its assault missions for the 5th and 24th Brigades in the European Theatre, as the Special Forces infiltration in the Gulf or in Ulster. In the Falklands, the only Chinook to escape the attack on the Atlantic conveyor carried out some memorable exploits well beyond the limits of the machine…

There is a peculiar RAF style amongst the crews composed of great coolness and strong professionalism. With the progressive retirement of the last Westland Wessex the fleet will essentially be composed of Chinooks and Puma as well as several Gazelles used for liaisons. With the new order of 14 Chinook in addition to the 35 already in service, the RAF is the second user of this type of machine in the world. All of them have been brought up to HC-2 standard and these extremely reliable machines have a long career. The Pumas have also been modernised and equipped for night operations that the RAF are particularly keen on. Even though they have kept their identification initials of HC-1, the Pumas currently in service have very little to do with the machines delivered at the beginning of the seventies. A new navigation system, Infrared jammers, a radar early warning system as well as chaffs launchers have been installed. A squadron of Puma or Chinook is composed of three flights, A, B and C, which in general have their own mission. For example, "A" Flight of a Puma squadron will be attached to missions of NATO's AMF Mobile Brigade. "B" Flight will operate in the UK and "C" Flight will be attached to the RAF Centre of Support and Development. Within a Chinook unit "A" and "B" Flights would work respectively for the 24th Airmobile Brigade whereas "C" Flight works for the Special Forces. It was during one of these secret flights that the Chiefs of Staff of the anti-terrorist branch were killed in a crash in Scotland in the spring of '95. In may 1995, with the announcement of the extra order of Chinooks, HM Government made clear its intention to acquire 22 EH-101SH (support helicopter) from 1999 which will replace the Puma. EH-101SH and Chinook HC-2 will continue to fly in British skies for the next two decades.

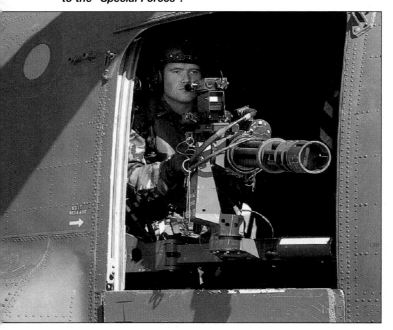

This Gatling gun at the door of a Chinook operating in Yugoslavia shows that the craft is attached to the "Special Forces".

A Chinook gets ready to transport a light Scorpion tank of the 5th brigade by sling during exercise BLUE LANYARD in Suffolk. The Chinook is the workhorse of the RAF.

Battle order:

Chinook: 7 Squadron, Odiham. 18 Squadron (mixed with Pumas), Laarbruch Germany. One detachment attached to Mount Pleasant's 78 Squadron, Falkland Islands.
Puma: 18 Squadron (mix with Chinooks), Laarbruch Germany. 33 Squadron, Odiham. 230 Sqn, Aldegrove, Ulster. Odiham based 27 Sqn is the Operational Conversion Unit (OCU) for Chinook and Puma pilots.
Wessex: 22 Squadron, St Mawgan. 60 Squadron, Benson. 72 Sqn, Aldegrove, Ulster. 84 Squadron, Akrotiri (Cyprus).
Some aircraft are also detached to Sea and Rescue Units (SAR) and schools (2 sqn FTU and RAF Central Flying School).
Gazelle: 32 Squadron, Northolt.

Current fleet:
Chinook HC-2: 35 (plus 14 in order).
Puma HC Mk1: 40.
Wessex: 62.
Gazelle MK3: 27.

The two types of RAF craft the Chinook and the Puma in action with the 24th airmobile brigade in the north of Germany.

49

GAZELLE HOT SA-342 M/L

The Gazelle hot has been, since 1980, the main anti-tank helicopter used in the three squadrons of every combat helicopter regiments of France's Army Aviation (ALAT). 200 machines designated SA-342 M were built and armed with four HOT A/T missiles capable of destroying a combat tank from more than 4000 metres. The sight is done by means of a "Viviane" firing telescope which could be operated at night. The HOT Gazelle is a type of "child of the cold war", where it had to use at any cost all the supports possible to install A/T missiles on it, so as to shatter the mass of Warsaw Pact tanks.

In order to compensate for the fragility of the cockpit, French pilots studied combat tactics based on mobility and concealment. The HOT Gazelles were engaged in the Gulf War and destroyed several Iraqi tanks during the advance of the Daguet division on Al Salman.

Cyprus, Egypt, Syria, Kuwait, the UAE, Iraq, Morocco and a large number of Arab countries also use the HOT Gazelle and some of these machines were engaged in various Near-East wars.

Above: Two Kuwaiti Gazelle above the desert. These craft destroyed several Iraqi tanks during the first few hours of the gulf war.

Below: A Gazelle of the 3rd RHC has just fired a HOT missile near Canjuers.

This Cypriot Gazelle HOT blends well into the near-desert landscape because of its camouflage.
In case of a clash with the Turkish forces the 4 Cypriot Gazelle could "assess" the situation because of their lightness and the familiar terrain.

BO-105 (ARMED)

A Swedish BO-105 hovering above a forest.
Armed with the HELITOW system the BO-105 is the principal Swedish antitank craft.

The small BO-105, known for its agility, is an excellent armament carrying platform. The Bundeswehr made it its principal anti-tank helicopter. The German Army call it the PAH-1 (PanzerAbwehr-Hub-Schrauber-1). The craft carries six HOT Euromissiles mounted on pods on each side of the fuselage. It is equipped with a firing sight placed on the roof of the cabin. The PAH-1 has encountered several modernisation programmes during its career. The first type was called PAH-1 A1 phase 1 and began its career in 1991and will see installation of new rotor blades and improvement of air inlets and the cooling system. Phase 2 of the PAH-1 program currently underway, will allow the BO-105 P to participate in night

This BO-105 is a machine capable of great agility as seen here with this dive.
Note the six HOT tubes on this German BO-105 from the regiment of antitank helicopters 32 based at Fritzlar.

A pilot of FAMET examines his BO-105 before leaving for an antitank mission as part of exercise IBERIA 93. The HOT missiles are not mounted during manoèuvres so as to allow extra fuel to be carried.

combat with the installation of an infrared firing sight and some new HOT-2 missiles mounted on lighter firing pods. The last modification envisaged is the conversion of 54 PAH-1 to the BSH standard (BegleitSchutz Hubschrauber) used as escort helicopters, armed with four air to air Stinger missiles. A BO-105/OPHELIA is currently being tested with a spherical observation mast. Spain, which built the BO-105 under license, uses also 28 BO-105, armed with HOT missiles with the name HA-15. The armed BO-105 is also in service, with the strength of 20 models, within the Swedish armed forces. Some of these machines, called BO-105 CBS, are equipped for A/T combat with the Esco Helitow System.

A BO-105 of the Bundeswehr taken just above the water during an infiltration exercise. The German BO-105 will be regrouped within new units attached to infantry divisions.

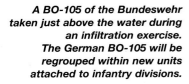

53

FAMET

With the rise of Islamic Fundamentalism, Spain found its place on the Mediterranean theatre of operation. Before the creation of FAMET (Fuerzas Aero-Môviles del Ejercito de Tierra), Spain only had a few UH-1B and Sikorski S-54 (used in the Western Sahara at the end of the sixties). FAMET is an important force capable of a rapid deployment of the 5th Airmobile Division, based at Corogne, where the Paracadaïsta of the BRIPAC are also stationed. These units often manoeuvre with their counterparts of the French or Italian Rapid Reaction Forces during exercises such as "Mistral" or "Tramontagne". The fleet of Spanish helicopters is fairly mixed but the acquisition of new Cougar as a replacement for the Bell UH-1 is a stage toward an improved standardisation of materials. The BO-105, sometimes armed with 20 mm guns and known locally as HA-15 or HR-15, is responsible for A/T combat and reconnaissance. Within FAMET, each type of craft is designed locally (see battle order below). Transport and heliborne assault missions are done by Bell UH-1 B, Cougar and Chinook. Despite an initial interest for the future NH-90 medium helicopter, Spain seems to be more interested in the Sikorski S-70 B (UH-60) to act as its future transport helicopter. No decision has yet been taken regarding the acquisition of a new attack helicopter.

During the Franco-Spanish exercise IBERIA, in the region of Mautauban, an antitank squadron equipped with HA-15 (alias BO-105) gets ready for take off.

Creating a whirlwind of straw and grass, these two Cougar have just transported French parachutists during exercise IBERIA 92.

The golden colour of the setting sun is reflected by this Bell UH-1H flying over the Sierra Nevada as part of exercise TRAMONTANA 94.

Battle order:

With its Headquarters (Jefatura de la Famet) based at Clomnier Viejo, the Spanish helicopter force is composed as follows:
1st "Batallon de Helicopteros de Ataque" (BHELA 1) at Almagro. Two A/T companies (1st and 2nd "Compania Contracarros") on HA-15 and HR-15.
2nd "Batallon de Helicopteros de Maniobras" (BHELMA II) at Betera. One "Compania de Transporte Medio" on HU-10B and one "Seccion de Reconocimiento" on HR-15 (Cougar in 1996).
3rd "Batallon de Helicopteros de Maniobras" (BHELMA III) at Agoncillo. One "Compania de Transporte Medio" on HU-10B and one "Seccion de Reconocimiento" on HR-15.
4th "Batallon de Helicopteros de Maniobras" (BHELMA IV) at El Copero. One "Compania de Transporte Medio" on HU-10B1 HU-21 and one "Seccion de Reconocimiento" on HR-15.
5th "Batallon de Helicopteros de Transporte" (BHELTA V) at Colemar Viejo. One "Compania de Transporte Medio" on HU-10B and one "Compania de Transporte Pesado" on HT-17.
6th "Batallon de Helicopteros de Canarias" (BHELCA VI) at Los Rodeos. One "Compania de Transporte Medio" on HU-10 B and one "Seccion de Reconocimiento" on HR-15. FAMET Flying School Centre based at Calomnier Viejo is equipped with HR-12 and HE-15.

Stock:
The local denomination of the machines is in brackets.
- Aerospatiale AS-532 Cougar (HU-21): 18 plus 18 ordered for 1996.
- Agusta Bell 212 (HU-18): 6
- Agusta Bell 206 A (HR 12-A): 5
- Bell OH-58 B (HR 12-B): 12
- Bell UH-1H (HU-10 B): 55
- Boeing CH-47 C/D Chinook (HT-17): 18
- CASA-MBB 105 (ATH HA-15): 46
- CASA-MBB 105 LOH (HR-15): 15
- CASA-MBB 105 CB training (HE-15): 11

This helmet of Spanish manufacture worn by an HA-15 pilot is not an imitation of a famous brand, even though it bears a well-known image.

Near Cordoue, this superb Chinook (alias HT-17) of the BHELTA V with sandy camouflage takes part in the Franco-Spanish exercise GALIA 89.

AGUSTA A-129 MANGUSTA

The prototype A-129 MANGUSTA was conceived at the request of the Italian army, who wanted an all-weather attack helicopter, equipped with a computerised control system, capable of night operation and of minimising crew tasks during combat missions. It flew for the first time on the 11th of September 1983. With the creation of this sophisticated machine, often called "Mini Apache", the transalpine aeronautical industry made a real technological leap. Production, however, was slowed down after the creation of five prototypes and the first standard machines were delivered to the ALE in July 1990, more than three years late.This delay was also due to the lack of funds available to buy the 80 Emerson-Saab Helitow weapons systems which were to equip the helicopters. 60 A-129 MANGUSTA were ordered to equip two attack squadrons.Barely in service, the MANGUSTAS were deployed in Somalia, as part of operation "Restore Hope" where they functioned very honourably. This craft can carry practically the whole range of western missiles or rocket launchers. On the other hand it has neither gun nor machine gun. ALE seems to prefer the MANGUSTA to be used in long range A/T combat. In spite of an extensive promotion campaign, the MANGUSTA was not a success as an export item. The Italian army recently ordered 30 models.

Armament details:

Each exterior pod is equipped with four carrying points able to rise 2 degrees or lower itself by 10 degrees in order to give maximum capacity to the firing shaft. In its ALE configuration, the MANGUSTA carries two Helitow systems, each one equipped with four TOW missiles as well as two 70 or 81mm rocket pods with a capacity of 19 or 7 rounds for each calibre. Guns or machine guns supports can be mounted. Mistral, Sidewinder, Stinger or Javelin missiles are an optional extra.

Baptism of fire for this Mangusta "war horse" which flies over Somalia during operation RESTORE HOPE. The rocket pod and 4 TOW missiles can be clearly made out under the aileron.

Characteristics

Crew: 2
Rotor diameter: 11,90 m
Length: 14,29 m
Height: 3,35 m
Engines: two Roll-Royce GEM 2 MK
each developing 825 hp
Weight: 2529 kg
Maximum take-off weight 4100 kg
Cruising speed: 250 km/h
Maximum speed: 315 km/h
Range: 100 m
Autonomy for a combat patrol:
90 minutes
Autonomy: 3 hrs

An angled take off for one of the first Mangusta delivered to the ALE at the Viterbe base.
Seen from the front this craft justifies its nickname of "mini Apache".

ITALIA. THE ALE
AVIAZIONE LEGGERA DEL ESERCITO

The collaboration between the flying machine and the infantry goes back to the Libyan War against the Ottomans, in 1911, when the Italians used aircraft for observation and support missions. No doubt purists concerning the tranalpines would see in that a distant forerunner of the ALE (AVIAZIONE LEGGERA DEL ESERCITO). This was officially created in 1959 after some difficulties with the Air Force who wanted to keep the monopoly on these aerial machines.

The first helicopters were the Bell AB-47 G and Sikorski S-55. Nowadays, ALE makes use of a varied stock, all the machines are constructed locally, as Agusta and Elicotteri Meridionali have acquired manufacturing licenses for the majority of models constructed by Bell. Reconnaissance and liaison are undertaken by AB-206 known as ERI-3 and by the A-109 A (ECI). The A-109 A serve as test machine for weapon system on the Mangusta and will operate from now on as a liaison helicopter. Italy was the first country,

after Russia and America, to develop an attack helicopter: the A-129 Mangusta (engaged in Somalia). Medium and heavy transport and helicopter assault missions are carried out by a fleet of AB-205, AB-212, AB-412 and CH-47 Chinook, used to tackling difficult situations. They have served in Mozambique, the Lebanon, Somalia, Namibia and in the Balkans during UN missions, during which ALE pilots were noted for their professional qualities.

With the exception of the Agusta A-109, all ALE helicopters can be armed with rocket pods, miniguns or a combination of MG-42/59 machine guns. In this case the suffix "A" for Armato is attached to its name.

The basic unit with the ALE is a squadron (squadrone) of six helicopters. Several squadrons form a gruppo Squadroni and several Gruppo Squadroni form a regiment. According to the traditions of the ALE the regiments bear a name of a constellation. Each corps of the army also has its ALE regiment: Aldebaran for the 3rd corps, Altair for the 4th Mountain corps and Rigel for the 5th corps. The famous Antares regiment with the Chinooks and AB-412 is the reserve of the Chief of Staff. There exist also independent and regional units or ones attached to special units such as the paras of the Folgore or the 9th Drago regiment, which operate on behalf of the special forces.

ALE will reach the next century with a force of 450 machines, in which the NH-90 should replace the AB-205 and the AB-212.

Seen at Viterbe a duo of AB-206 which are the principal scouts of the ALE.

A war like situation for this Mangusta A-129 at the airport at Mogadishu.

Battle order:

Centro ALE at Viterbo: A-109, AB-205, AB-206, AB-412.

1st Reggimento ALE Antares in the region of Viterbe: 11 Gruppo squadroni ETM Ercole with 111, 112 and 121 squadroni ETM on CH-47 C Chinook.

51 Gruppo squadroni EM Meone with 511 and 512 squadroni EM on AB-412.

3rd Reggimento ALE Aldebaran in the Milanese: 46 Gruppo squadroni EA Sagittario with 461 and 462 squadroni AE on A-129 Mangusta.

53 Gruppo squadroni EM Cassiopea with 531, 532, 533 squadroni EM on AB-205 and 423 squadrone ERI on AB-206 plus Sezione Elicotteri da Collegamento on AB-412. 4th Reggimento ALE Altair in the Alps made up of the 34th Gruppo squadroni Toro, 44th Gruppo squadroni Fenice and 54 Gruppo squadroni Cefeo which includes the following units: 440th, 441st and 442nd squadrone ERI on AB-206. 541st, 542nd, 543rd, 544th and 545th squadrone EM on AB-205.

5th Reggimento ALE Rigell en Vénitie including the 25th gruppo Squadroni Cigno, 49th gruppo squadrone Capricorno and 55th gruppo squadroni Dragone which has the following units: 425th and 481st squadroni ALE on AB-205 and AB-206, 551st, 552nd and 553rd squadrone EM on AB-205.

492nd squadrone ERI on A-109, 491 squadronie EA on A-129, 493 squadrone EM on AB-412.

Independent units: 20th gruppo squadroni Andromeda at Salerno with the 420 squadrone ERI (AB-206 and 520 squadroni EM (AB-212)

21st gruppo squadroni Orsa Maggiore at Cagliari with the 421st and 422nd squadroni ERI (AB-206) and 515th squadrone EM (AB-205)

26th Gruppo Squadroni Giove at Pisa with the 426th and 526th squadroni ERI (AB-206)

27th Gruppo Squadroni Mercurio at Florence with the 427th squadroni ERI (AB-206)

28th Gruppo Squadroni Tucano at Rome with 428th squadroni ERI (AB-206) and the sezione Elicotteri da Collgamento (A-109),

30th Gruppo squadroni Pegaso at Catania with 430th squadrone ERI (A-109 A) and 530th squadrone EM (AB-212) 39th Gruppo squadroni Drago with 391st squadrone ERI (A-109).

Abbreviations:

EA : Elicottero d'Attacco
EM : Elicottero Multiruolo.
ETM: Elicottero da transporte Medio.
ERI : Elicottero da Ricognizione.

Opposite from top to bottom:
An A-109 HIRUNDO used for liaison at Viterbe.

AB-205 of the 4th regiment ALTAIR.

Chinook from the famous Antares regiment which saw action in Mozambique, Lebanon and Yugoslavia.

An AB-412 which will without doubt be the medium helicopter of ALE throughout the next decade.

MIL MI-24 HIND

The appearance of this soviet combat helicopter was, for NATO, a clap of thunder in an otherwise blue sky. It was indeed the case that, until the beginning of the seventies, the Atlantic Alliance had a clear superiority in the area of aeromobility. The introduction of MiL-Mi 24 (code name HIND) into the Red Army spread a wave of panic amongst the western Chiefs of Staff. In spite of obvious good qualities, the Red monster was, without doubt, overestimated. The Mi-24 was also the symbol of soviet expansionism and the nightmare of all anticommunist guerrillas since the Russian attack helicopter fought in Angola, Afghanistan, Ethiopia and in Nicaragua. It had a reputation for invincibility up until the delivery of Stinger missiles in Afghanistan by the Reagan administration.

Basically the Mi-24 was developed as an armoured troop transport and could assure its own protection. The MIL office rapidly transformed its project into a real flying tank. Powered by the two same TV-2 117A engines that already were part of the Mi-8, the Hind had an armoured cabin and two wings equipped with equipment fixation points. The prototype flew in 1970 and the first standard Mi-24 A machines were delivered to the soviet forces in Germany in 1973 with AT-SWATTER anti-tank missiles. The first Type A Mi-24 had a vast glass cockpit and the pilots were side by side. A Mi-24 B version, equipped with a Gazelle type tail, flew but was not followed up.

The Mi-24 was a training version. Combat experience showed that transport of troops damaged the offensive performance of the Mi-24 which gradually abandoned this role to the more agile Mi-8 in order to dedicate itself entirely to support fire. The combat in Afghanistan emphasised the vulnerability of the crews in the "Glass" cockpit; also the nose of the craft was entirely redesigned and the pilot and gunner found themselves equipped with a plexiglass bubble. A chin turret equipped with four tube of 14.5mm canons firing 4000 rounds per minute was added to this new version christened Mi-24 Hind D by NATO. Scarcely begun in service in the Red Army, the Hind D was replaced by the Mi-24 V Hind-E equipped with a launching rail for Spiral AT-6 missiles. The Russians exported this model under the name Mi-35. To stand up the Stinger, the Mi-24 V was covered with an Infrared jamming device, chaff launchers and even a system to reduce the thermal signature; all that at the expense of the performance.

In Afghanistan, the 12,7 mm calibre proved to be insufficient to attain certain objectives. As a consequence a new version of the helicopter made its appearance, the

Two Czech MI-24 equipped with a superb shark's mouth taking off from the Ceske Budovice base during a meeting.
In the Czech republic this craft is called "Krokodil".

On a Russian base, one of the latest versions of the MIL flying tank, the MI-24 P "HIND F" easily recognisable by its two GSH-30 30 mm guns on the right under the cockpit.

Mi-24 P Hind-F whose right side under the cockpit was equipped with two twinned 30 mm canons with a capacity of 750 rounds. These machines are used in mixed formation with former models. The least well known version of the Hind is without doubt the model Mi-24 Rch Hind-G, a craft designed for chemical, nuclear and bacteriological reconnaissance. Equipped with multiple captors, this version was seen during the Chernobyl disaster. There is also a photographic reconnaissance version, adapted to artillery fire range, the Mi-24 K Hind-G 2. The Soviet monster has now been demystified but the Hind remains a formidable war machine, even if it is slightly underpowered. At the last Paris Air Show in 1995, MIL presented the Mi-35 M, a modernised version, equipped with French avionics, which could interest a number of users of the Mi-24.

Because of the large amount of military material available in the east after the fall of communism, many countries have been able to equip themselves with a reasonable combat helicopter force such as this Croatian MI-24 successfully engaged in offensives in 1995 in Krajina.

Characteristics

HIND-D

Rotor diameter: 17,30 m
Length: 19,79 m
Height: 6,50 m
Engines:
2 Klimov (Isotov) turbines TV-3-117
developing each 2200 hp
Weight: 8400 kg
Weight with full load:
12500 kg
Cruising speed: 260 km/h
Maximum speed: 310 km/h
Range: 750 km with auxiliary tank
Armament: fixed armament can vary
depending on the versions
but the Mi-24 wings authorised
fixation for a wide range
of rockets, A/T missiles AT-2 Swatter,
AT-6 Spiral or AA IGLA.

PZL SWIDNIK W-3 SOKOL

With the acquisition of the manufacturing licence of the Mi-2 Hoplite, the Polish company PZL Swidnick, had gained enough experience to launch the construction of its own machines. The outline is not very attractive, but its robustness brings to mind the initial model, the Mi-2. The W-3 SOKOL (Falcon) has larger dimensions and reexamined aerodynamics. The first of the five prototypes flew on the 16th of November 1979 and production began in 1985. The SOKOL can carry 12 soldiers who are

able to disembark via two large side doors. The first six machines were delivered to the 47th Helicopter Regiment at Nowe Miasto and Burma acquired 12 models. A combat and ground support version were also developed under the name W-3WB HUZA. This name does not refer to a single machine but to the whole ensemble of Polish combat helicopters destined to reinforce the 29 Mi-24 D/V that Poland has. A radom permitting AT-6 ATGM Spiral missiles to be fired is mounted under the nose of the craft, and carries on four support points two 80mm ten round rocket pods and 8 Spiral missile launchers, in a classic configuration. Platan mine droppers, AA-SAM-7 missiles, as well as four Grom A/T missiles, the local version of the Russian Igla missile, can also be mounted. Fixed weaponry consists of two 23mm Gsh-23 guns mounted on the right of the fuselage, under the cockpit, as in the later version of the Mi-24. A lighter attack version, but with no anti-tank capacity, the W-3 W Salamander, entered into service in the form of ten models for the 47th Helicopter Combat Regiment. There is no doubt that the W-3 WB will be the backbone of the new Polish airmobile brigade which should include about a hundred helicopters.

A Polish soldier gets ready to embark a Salamander W-3W of the 47th aviation regiment which is landing at Biedrowsko during a NATO exercise.

A Salamander of the 47th Rgt of aviation, reminiscent of the MI-2. Note the two 23 mm guns.

Characteristics

W-3 Sokol

Rotor diameter: 15,70 m
Length: 14,21 m
Height: 4,12 m
Engines:
2 WSK-PZL Rzeszow
TWD-10W turbines
developing each 900 hp
Weight: 3300 kg
Weight with full load:
6400 kg
Cruising speed:
235 km/h
Maximum speed:
270 km/h
Range: 1225 km

At Poznan, during exercise Cooperative Bridge. These W-3 SOKOL have a brilliant camouflage.

PZL SWIDNIK MI-2 HOPLITE

In January 1964, during the Cold War, the Soviets signed an agreement with Poland, allowing the PZL company exclusivity of manufacture and sales of the light Mi-2 helicopter which had made its first flight in January 1964. Since 1955, the Polish firm had already built 1700 Mi-1 Hare.

The Mi-2 nicknamed Hoplite by NATO was the workhorse of the Warsaw Pact: light support, liaison, observation, artillery control, casevac, and VIP transport were among its most common missions.

More than 5250 Mi-2 were built and exported until the end of production in 1991. A lot of this small, unattractive yet efficient helicopter remain in service.

An MI-2 "Hoplite" with very exotic markings as it belongs to the small air force of Djibouti.
These craft equipped with makeshift weaponry, were engaged in combat against the Affars rebellion.

AH-64 A/B APACHE

The Apache became a legend on the night of 17 January 1992, firing Hellfire missiles on an Iraqi radar shelter. The story of this fantastic combat helicopter starts at the beginning of the seventies, when the Pentagon asked several manufacturers to develop an attack helicopter capable of operating on the front line at night and during any weather conditions. The manufacturers Bell and Hughes were selected to conceive two prototypes. After an intensive evaluation the AH-64 A Hughes prototype, which had made its maiden flight on 30 September 1975, was chosen. Several more prototypes were then built and on 26 March 1982 the US Army signed a first contract for 11 models. With the acquisition of Hughes by McDonnell Douglas in 1985, the helicopter changed its name to become the McDonnell Douglas AH-64 A Apache. Two-seater, in tandem, the Apache is an ultra-sophisticated machine offering a maximum of protection to its crew, in terms of electronic counter-measures or simple armour. The results were yet more encouraging as during the Gulf war only six Apache were lost. The entire power of the Apache is in the nose which houses the avionics, and in the Martin-Marietta AN/AAQ-11 TADS/PNVS (Target Acquisition and Designation Sight/Pilot Night Vision Sensor) armament control system. This system consists of a surveillance camera observing the battlefield, a laser indicator, a laser range-finder, and everything linked to a navigation system which shows the position of both the helicopter and the enemy to the crew, in daytime and at night. During combat, the Apache, which can be helped by the Scout OH-58, flies very close to the ground following its contours and is included in a complete weapons system which can even include "A 10 tank killer" aeroplanes. The majority of vitals of the craft are protected against 25mm projectiles, the standard AA artillery of the ex-Warsaw pact armies, and the crew has a 95% chance of survival during a crash at low altitude.

The weaponry consists of a 30mm chain gun supplied with 1200 rounds and, of course, 16 AGM-11 A4 "Hellfire" 3 missiles. The Apache also carries 70mm Hydra rocket pods. Even though air to air combat is not really envisaged in the doctrine of the US Army, the Apache can carry AA Sidewinder, Stinger and even Mistral missiles. Six Apaches can be transported in a Galaxy, two in a C-141 and three in a new C-17, which proves the importance given by the Americans to strategic transport. The symbol of American technology, the Apache had its baptism of fire during operation "Just Cause" in Panama, as part of the 82nd Airborne. During the Gulf war the craft proved that it was an essential element of the

The strange silhouette of this Apache contrasts with the purity of the Saudi desert. Here a machine of the 1/82 "Wolfpack" one of the antitank units of the aviation brigade of the 82nd Airborne was seen during "DESERT SHIELD".

American arsenal. While waiting for the AH-64 D/Longbow Apache, the US Army used 813 machines and the craft was also sold to the Allied nations. Winner of the "deal of the century" against the Tiger, the Super Cobra and the Rooival, the Apache in its AH-64D version, has just been selected by the Netherlands and Britain.

On the warpath, an Apache of the 1/3 belonging to the 2nd Armoured division takes off from a clearing near Wurzburg in Germany.

Characteristics

Rotor diameter: 14.63m
Length: 17.76m
Height: 4.66m
Engines:
two General Electric turbines
T-700 GE-701 each
developing 1800 hp.
Empty weight: 5165kg
Weight with full load: 9525kg
Capacity: 1157 l plus 771 l in tank
Maximum speed: 365 km/h
Cruising speed: 293 km/h
Range: 1701 km

Above: Close up of an Apache of the 5/6 aviation rgt based at Wiesbaden and displaying all its power with its 25 mm gun, Hydra 70 mm rocket pods as well as different sensors in the nose.

The middle east has proved to be a good market for the Apache with several large orders from pro-western emirates as well as Israel. Here, a rare sight, an Israeli AH-64 at the Ramon base in the Neguev.

US. ARMY

The Americans are not, in fact, the real inventors of the helicopter, yet their spirit of initiative and their technology have given such an impulse to the concept of airmobility that, nonetheless, they have an incontestable leadership in this domain. The land of the pioneers, the US welcomed Prof. Piasecki and Prof.

Sikorsky, eminent Russian scientists, who sought refuge, at the beginning of the twenties, from the October revolution. They had constructed some rather strange flying machines for the army of the Tsar. The impetus was started and, from the end of the second world war, the first American helicopters began service in the Army. Helicopter combat, both supple and flexible, was tested in Korea and developed in Vietnam. The methods used by the US Army and the training of helicopter elite troops were proof of success for the US. It was not without reason that the first great American airmobile unit took the name of the first CAV dear to the memory of every American patriot. With more than 7430 helicopters in service, the US Army is, of course, the greatest user of them in the world. American pilots use the following machines: OH-58 C/D and OH-6A for observation, AH-IS Cobra and AH-64A for attack and antitank combat, UH-1 for servitude and light transport and UH-60 A/C and CH-47 for helicopter assaults and heavy transport. Each division has its aviation brigade with a hundred helicopters. Depending on whether it is Light, Air Assault, Airborne or Heavy, the structure of the units can be slightly modified.

The small yet sophisticated OH-58 D has replaced the "Loach" of Vietnam. Here a Kiowa and its " ball" belonging to the 4th aviation regiment of the 8th ID.

Cobra of the 11th Cavalry Regiment. The collaboration with the tanks is evident. The 11th ACAV was for a long time the guardian of the iron curtain in the strategic sector of Fulda. As for all the ACAV, the 11th has a squadron of combat helicopters.

A squadron of helicopters of the 1/3 aviation regiment of the 2nd US armoured division take off for an attack mission. These craft are leaving a FARP (Forward Air Refuelling Point) at least 12 kilometres from the front where they are refuelled and rearmed.

It is generally composed of:
- an airborne cavalry squadron responsible for recognising and testing the enemy (16 OH-58 and 16 AH-1S),
- an attack battalion of 24 or 48 Apache and 24 OH-58D destined to "break" the enemy,
- an assault battalion of forty or so Blackhawk, three of which are electronic war.

The mission of this last battalion is, of course, assault transport. The US army underwent budgetary reductions and very many prestigious divisions such as the 1st and 2nd Armoured division or the Victory division (24th mechanised) were disbanded. There remain currently 10 active divisions but very many units of the National Guard have helicopter units. Each corps of the army (currently four) has an aviation brigade equipped with more than 300 machines. These brigades are comprised of a commanding battalion, three assault battalions (UH-60), four attack battalions (AH-64), a medium transport battalion (CH-47) and a liaison battalion.

Lastly, there are many independent units: an aviation brigade, a theatre of operation brigade, training and assessment units, electronic warfare units, medical helicopter units and the top secret 160th Special operations regiment. For the beginning of the 21st century the

An Apache pilot of the 5/6 Aviation regiment, like all pilots everywhere, inspects his craft before a mission. The chain gun is clearly visible.

Pentagon hopes to standardise its stock of helicopters which will use only four types of craft, UH-64D, OH-38D (while waiting for the futuristic RAH-66 Comanche), the UH-60C and the tireless Chinook in its CH-47D version. From a technological point of view the US army remains none other than a giant at the end of this century.

US. ARMY

Battle order:

A small book would be necessary to give
a detailed battle order of the US Army
so we have limited ourselves
to the large units without going into the subdivisions.
1st Corps: 66th Aviation Brigade.
Fort Lewis, Wisconsin.
III Corps: 6th Aviation Brigade, Fort Hood, Texas.
VIII Corps (Airborne): 18th Aviation Brigade.
Fort Bragg North Carolina.
V Corps: 12th Aviation Brigade, Germany.
Divisions of aviation Brigades:
1st Infantry Division (mech). Big Red One.
Wurzburg, Germany.
2nd Infantry Division (mech). Camp Red Cloud Korea.
3rd Infantry Division (mech). Fort Stewart, Georgia.
4th Infantry Division (mech). Fort Hood, Texas.
10th Mountain Division (light). Fort Drum, New York.
25th Infantry (light) Hawaii.
1st Cavalry Division. Fort Hood, Texas.
1st Armoured Division Bad Kreuznach, Germany.
82nd Airborne Division. Fort Bragg, North Carolina.

These Bell UH-1 attached to the NATO command have just landed a Chief of Staff during exercise Certain Strike. The end of the century will doubtless see the withdrawal of this helicopter which has marked the history of airmobility.

101st Air Assault Division Fort Campbell Kentucky.
Reserve units also have helicopter units: 24th(mech),
28th (Armd), 29th (light), 34th (mech), 35th (mech),
38th (mech), 40th (mech), 42nd (Armd).

These BlackHawk UH-60 of the aviation brigade of the 1st US Armoured division take off from a terrain in Germany after boarding infantrymen.

In the pale light of a German winter, a CH-47 of the Vth US Corps has just put a crashed Huey on the trailer of a lorry, during REFORGER 85.

Units in theatres of operations:
Alaska: 123rd AvnBn.
Germany: 6th Avn Co, 207th Avn Co, 502nd Avn Co.
Korea: 17th Aviation Brigade South west Asia.
Fort Benning Panama: 128th Avn Brigade.
Fort Campbell: 160th Special Operation Regiment:
Two companies A and B on MH and OH-6, three battalions 1-160, 2-160, 3-160 on M-60 and M-H-47, an independent battalion 1-245 (MH-60 MH-47, UH-1H) and 617th SOA Det. There are 56 independent medical aviation companies (Aeromed Co) on UH-1V or UH-60 and 12 Combat Enhancing Capability Aviation Team (CECAT), assessment and technical research company on UH-1H.
Training is conducted at Fort Rucker, Alabama, within the Aviation Training Brigade which has in supply all models of machines used in the US Army

Stock: 73 AH-1 S Cobra,
754 AH-64A Apache,53 AH-6/MH-6,
2780 Bell UH-1H, 3 EH-1H (ECM),
1216 UH/MH-60 A/C BlackHawk,
66 EH-60 A (ECM),
90 OH-6A Cayuse, 1543OH-58 A/C Kiowa, 335 OH-58 D,
455 CH/MH-47 Chinook,
29 TH-67 Creek. (These figures also include craft of the National Guard).

THE GULF WAR

Chemical decontamination for a Cobra of the 82nd Airborne during the preliminary phase of the war when the allies feared a chemical attack.

On 2 August 1990, Kuwait city was besieged by an Iraqi helicopter assault remarkably led by Mi-8s, backed up by Mi-24s linked to a tank attack. Several Kuwaiti Gazelle had attempted a last ditch struggle by destroying several tanks with HOT missiles before seeking refuge in Saudi Arabia. Powerful America reacted almost immediately and, from the end of the month of August, the Paras of the 82nd Airborne were deployed with Apache, Cobra, Kiowa and Bell from their helicopter brigade. In the following months, there was an impressive increase in power of the US forces with the arrival of the 101st Air Assault division, aviation brigades of the 24th mechanised division, the 1st Infantry division, the 2nd and 3rd armoured division, the 1st Cavalry division as well as the Chinook units of the VII and XVIII corps to which are added the squadrons of the airborne cavalry of the 2nd and 3rd Regiments of armoured cavalry. In other words more than a thousand helicopters.

The RAF and the RAAC sent Pumas, Chinooks, Gazelles and Lynxes while the French ALAT was operational in the region of Hafar el Battim with both Gazelles and Pumas.

It was, of course, the Apache which became the superstar of the Gulf war by destroying radar sites on the night of 17 January 1991. Several days before the land assault, some Apaches of the 101st Air Assault took more than 500 prisoners, simply by manifesting themselves.

Rafah, February 1992, this photo can be considered historic. The Apache with the shark's mouth of the 101st Air assault has just destroyed two vehicles and taken 320 prisoners. With the rotor turning it is resupplied before returning to where it is needed. For the first time ever a helicopter has captured an infantry battalion.

Prisoners were otherwise evacuated by CH-47 Chinook. During the land offensive, the omnipresent Apaches destroyed 81 tanks and 23 armoured vehicles and contributed to the capture of 3200 Iraqi soldiers.

6 Apache were lost and sadly some craft were implicated in two incidents between the allied forces.

Chinooks were also widely used for bringing fuel to leading armoured units as well as ammunition for the MLRS multiple rocket launchers. For the return journey, the large bi-turbines were filled with Iraqi prisoners. Adapting their tactics to the desert, the ALAT Gazelle had the responsibilities of the cavalry to destroy, the majority of the time, tanks abandoned by their crew, which takes nothing away from the courage and valour of the French pilots. The RAF used several of its Chinooks, specially modified, to penetrate into Iraqi territory so SAS troops could carry out their mission of reconnaissance and destruction of SCUD missiles. Saddam Hussein had a not insignificant helicopter force but never used them in battle and clearly wanted to save them.

Training flight above the desert for these BlackHawk of the 2/82 "Corsair". A night time vigil in the gulf for these Chinook of the XVIIIth Corps.

Used well, the Mi-24, BO-105 gun and Gazelle could have inflicted severe losses to the coalition forces but clearly the majority of these machines did not take to the air.

A prisoner of the Iraqis, I was evacuated by helicopter to Baghdad after a week's captivity at Bassorah. Our Bell 212 "borrowed" from the UN had to refuel at the Kut base. To my great surprise I saw there approximately 50 intact Mi-24, Mi-8, Gazelle and BO-105 lined up as if on parade and in perfect condition.

For a number of observers, the Gulf war, apart from the first days, seemed to be only half a war.

Capable of deploying 9 infantry battalions and of backing them up, the 101st Air Assault division is a unique formation, as much for its flexibility of use as for its material which was perfectly adapted to air combat. The unit based at Fort Campbell, Kentucky, is comprised of three airmobile infantry brigades, of an artillery brigade with four battalions and auxiliary battalions, all this backed up by a strong aviation brigade (see chart). The Gulf war proved the know-how of the "Screaming Eagle" which "opened the show" on the 17 January 1991 when the "Task Force Normandy" consisting of 8 Apache destroyed Iraqi defence radars 700km behind enemy lines. 27 Hellfire missiles, 100 70mm rockets 4000 30mm rounds fired in two minutes from a distance of 3 to 6 km pulverised the enemy shelters, thus creating a pathway for the aircraft. On the return trip, a Chinook "Fat Cow" refuelled in the middle of the desert. After a journey of 1750km and 15 hours in enemy territory, Apaches and Chinooks, the latter damaged by a missile, returned to their base. During land operations the 101st launched a helicopter assault of 2000 men transported by 100 BlackHawk and Chinook. This operation allowed the crea-

A Cobra of the "Screaming Eagles" in the gulf. The tritube 20 mm gun, the TOW missiles, the rocket launchers and behind the rotor block the "Magic Lantern" for luring possible IR missiles are all clearly visible on this photo.

Having been refuelled this Apache of the 101st Air Assault division, heavily armed with 8 Hellfires and rocket pods will return to combat in the gulf. Note the large extra tank under the left wing.

"SCREAMING EAGLES"

*A UH-60 L, latest and very effective version of the BlackHawk,
takes off from Fort Campbell, Kentucky.*

tion of a zone named Cobra, 80km
inside Iraq, which was used as a
base for Cobras and Apaches of the
division, during many "Search and
Destroy" operations. These events
show the value of the airmobile
concept when it is carried out by a
formation having both the experience and the means of the 101st Air
Assault Division.

**Units forming
the aviation brigade
of the 101st Air Assault Division:**
2/17 Cav Squadron with OH-58D
6-101 General Support Aviation Bn
with UH-60 and EH-60D.
7-101 Medium Hel Bn with CH-47D.
4-101 Assault Hel Bn with UH-60.
5-101 Assault Hel Bn with UH-60.
9-101 Assault Hel Bn with UH-60.
1-101 Attack Hel Bn with AH-64.
2-101 Attack Hel Bn with AH-64.
3-101 Attack Hel Bn with AH-64,
or 54 AH-64, 63 OH-58 D,
125 UH-60, 3 EH-60, 45 CH-47 D.

*At Fort Campbell, a Chinook of the 7/101 is
winching up a Hummer Avenger, a version of the
famous antiaircraft vehicle equipped with Stinger.*

73

KAMOV KA-50 "HOKUM"

The appearance of the Apache led the Russians to develop a new generation of attack helicopters in order to replace the formidable Mi-24. Two models were chosen, the Mil Mi-28 "Havoc" and the Kamov KA-50 "Hokum". It was the latter that was officially selected but it seems that the Mi-28 were operational within several units of the Russian army.

The Russians maintain that the Kamov KA-50 "Hokum", under its NATO name, will be the best attack helicopter at the end of this century. Whereas the Mil bureau was directed towards a classical formula similar to the American AH-64 in the competition for a new combat machine for the Red Army, Sergei Mikheyev, general engineer at Kamov, was working on his own concept. Thinking that the anticouple rotor, common to all helicopters, damaged its performance and proved to be very vulnerable during combat, the Russian engineer retained the formula of two contra-rotating rotors placed on a thin fuselage. All this technological experience was put into the conception of a new combat helicopter, the prototype of which was named V-80, and which took its maiden flight on 27 July 1982. Kamov won the competition. A new generation of armament equipped the craft and particularly the laser guided missile Vikhr. The load during wartime equipped with a proximity rocket is capable of penetrating 900mm of armour and the missile is launched beyond the reach of the majority of western anti-air capabilities. Even though the Hokum can carry all types of air to air missile, the Vikhr missile, thanks to its proximity rocket, can also be fired against aircraft. The 16 Vikhr missiles can also be replaced or completed by AS-12 "Kegler" guided missiles or B-8 80mm rocket pods. The gun placed on the right is the very well known 30mm 2A42.

The survival during combat is increased by infrared suppressors in the exhaust, by the armoured and pressurised cockpit and by self-sealing tanks.

The Hokum even had an ejectable seat Severin/Zveda K-37. The ejection sequence started by the automatic dissociation of the rotors and the fuselage before the explosion of the door and the expulsion of the pilot.

The "Werewolf", in menacing black, takes part in a demonstration at Bourget air show. This model, without doubt, foreshadows the helicopters of the next century.

Equipped with the famous contra-rotating rotor, as tested on KAMOV marine helicopters, the HOKUM, heavily armoured and loaded with electronics, is considered by the Russians to be the best attack helicopter in the world.

Characteristics

Rotor diameter: 14.50 m
Length: 16 m
Height: 5.40 m
Engines: Two Klimov Isotov TV3 117VK turbines developing 1660 hp
Weight with full load: 7500 kg
Maximum speed: 350 km/h
Mission radius: 250 km

MIL MI-28 HAVOC

The first of three prototypes flew on the 10 November 1982, it was a classic configuration assault helicopter with armoured glass, chin gun and armament pods. The tail rotor is distinguishable by its two propellers with two independent blades forming a very narrow X.

Fixed armaments consist of a 30mm monotube 2A 42 gun. This is mounted under the nose and resupplied by two ammunition boxes each containing 150 rounds. Each of the four pylons mounted under the fin can carry a military load of 480kg constituted mainly of 4 AT-6 "Spiral" launchers or various rocket pods. The chaff launchers are found at the end of the fins. The nose contains a battlefield surveillance camera, a rangefinder and a laser designator. The craft can fly and fight at night. The cockpit is protected by a titanium and ceramic armour and all the vital elements of the craft are lined and protected by an armour plate. The crew seats are designed to absorb the shock of a descent of 12m/s and, in the case of major problems, explosive bolts tear open the doors while a slide inflates along the length of the fuselage allowing the crew to evacuate from the craft without the risk of touching the rotors.

This front view of a HAVOC shows us its rather unattractive silhouette, however the many bumps house sophisticated equipment.

This prototype of the HAVOC presented at the Bourget air show lives up to its name of the Russian Apache. The camouflage is experimental.

Characteristics

Rotor diameter: 17.20 m
Length: 19;15 m
Engines: Two Klimov Isotov
TV-3 - 117 turbines
each developing 2200 hp
Empty weight: 7000 kg
Weight with full load: 10400 kg
Fuel: 1900 l giving
2 hours endurance and
an autonomy of 470 km
Maximum speed: 300 km/h
Cruising speed: 270 km/h

EUROCOPTER HAC TIGER/PAH-1 TIGER

With this Franco-German model, which should enter service in the year 2000, the Bundeswehr and ALAT will have created a real technological bond. Born out of necessity as a result of the German need to find a replacement for the PAH-2 (BO-105 HOT), the programme proved interesting to France which was considering a successor to the Gazelle HOT. Five prototypes were realised by Aerospatiale in France and MBB in Germany. The first one flew at Marignane on 29 April 1991. The craft was entirely constructed of composite materials. All electrical, hydraulic and fuelling systems were doubled or tripled. This contributed greatly to the survival of the machine. An MIL-STD 1553 computer integrated in the avionics and the different weapon systems permitted the crew to devote their time to tactical operations and piloting. The HAC antitank version is built around the new TRIGAT "Fire and Forget" missile carried at the rate of eight. The Osiris mast sight coupled to a thermal camera and a battlefield observation screen permitted the eight missiles to be fired sheltered from the view of the enemy and indeed enemy fire.

For its AA protection, the Tiger can carry Mistral or Stinger missiles. France chose an HAP version armed with a 30mm GUN, two SNEB 68mm rocket pods and 4 Mistrals, whereas the Germans preferred to develop the UH multi-role version, armed with a 20mm gun and rockets.

Characteristics

Rotor diameter: 13 m
Length: 14 m
Engines: Two MTU/Turbomeca /Rolls Royce MTR 390 turbines each developing 1285 hp
Empty weight: 3300 kg
Weight with full load: 600 kg
Fuel capacity: 1360 l
Maximum speed: 280 km/h
Cruising speed: 250 km/h
Endurance: 3 and a half hours.

This Tiger, one of the HAP version French prototypes equipped with a 30 mm gun, makes a test flight near Marignane. The machine is "electronically" protected from the many dangers of the battlefield.

A flight over Bavaria for this Untersstützungshubschrauber equipped with the most sophisticated prototype weapons. Note the Osiris mast viewfinder.

ATLAS CSH-2 ROOIVALK

Diplomatically isolated and subject to an arms embargo for two decades, the Republic of South Africa created its own large and very reliable armaments industry. The Rooivalk is one of the fruits of this enterprise. The development of a local attack helicopter started in 1981 with the construction of the XH-1 Alpha prototype followed by the XTP-2 Beta, which eventually gave rise to the first Rooivalk prototype (red falcon) named XH-2 and which was rapidly transformed into CSH-2 (combat support helicopter). In spite of its futuristic appearance, the Rooivalk kept its Turbomeca Turbo IV and the Puma rotor which was and remains the standard helicopter of the SAAF. The engines are positioned on the side of the fuselage so that the two crew members, positioned in tandem in an anti-reflective cockpit, have better visibility. The chin turret uses a target detector and a system composed of a laser range finder, a navigation and night-firing system and a TV camera which follows the helmet movements of the members of the crew. The cockpit is adapted to use night vision glasses and all missions in all weather/day or night are facilitated by the existence of two computers, one of which helps to sight the weapon and the other to navigate with the aid of maps appearing on a screen. The Rooivalk is powerfully armed with an Armscor GA-1 Ratler 20mm gun which will possibly be replaced by a turret containing a DEFA 533 30mm gun. This fixed weapon can be completed by various vectors carried under four pylons, 68mm, 18 round rocket launchers or Atlas Swift antitank missiles. Well protected by armour the Rooivalk also carried infrared scramblers and electronic counter-measure equipment. It is likely that the standard versions will differ slightly from the prototype. An unfortunate competitor of the well-known British and Dutch attack helicopter programmes, the Rooivalk also suffered as a result of the reduction of the South African military budget and only 12 models (representing a squadron) were ordered by the SAAF. A middle Eastern country would also be interested by this technologically advanced craft but will doubtless have some problems putting it on the market against the omnipresent and well-proven AH-64 Apache.

Flagship of South African industry, the Rooivalk is a machine both simple and sophisticated, developed from the experience of combat of the South Africans during the war in Angola.

One of the prototypes of the Rooivalk test fires its 30 mm gun.

Characteristics

Rotor diameter: 15.08 m
Engines: Two Atlas Turbomeca Turmo IV Topaz
Normal weight at take off: 7200 kg
Weight with full load: 8000 kg
Maximum speed: 315 km/h
Cruising speed: 269 km/h
Autonomy: 940 km with reserve tanks: 1335 km.

ATTACK HELICOPTERS

The Marines invented airmobile combat when they launched their large Sikorsky S-55 for a hill assault in Korea. This was perfected by the French in Algeria who established the doctrines of combat. From that point onwards the vertical encircling movement became a reality and officer parachutists, often victims of the whims of the wind, threw themselves into airmobile combat. Paradoxically, the helicopter, during a classic airborne assault, permitted freedom from the restrictions of the weather, enabled a swift organisation and the avoidance of dispersion and long regroupments as in the OAP which often gave the enemy time to react or flee. From then on helicopters and elite troops made a good team and in Vietnam the battle of the River Drang saw an entire division, the First Cav, lead a succession of airmobile operations throughout a whole week with its support fire coming from the sky and its artillery used by sky cranes. The combat in Vietnam is indissociable from the Huey in its B version which will progressively be brought up to the UH-1H standard, the most flexible and widespread helicopter in the world. All five continents will see generations of soldiers descend from the Hueys to track the Vietcong, the CT (Communist terrorist or "Charlie") or the subservisos and penetrate the jungle, protected by the gunships, armed with M-60 miniguns or 40mm grenade launchers. The UH-1H was to improve considerably and the descendants of the Huey machines used at the time of Vietnam have really nothing to do with their illustrious predecessor apart from a vaguely similar silhouette. The seventies and the eighties saw the generalisation of helicopter operations. Syrian assaults on Mount Hermon and Egyptian assaults in the Sinai during the October war, counter guerrillas in Central America and the bush war in southern Africa with the intensive use of the Alouette III and Puma. The Soviets are not behind and launch their Mi-8's, Mi-17's supported by the Mi-24's in Afghanistan and later in Tchetchenie. In the west, NATO is to considerably reduce the number of tanks, which became useless after the end of the Warsaw pact, to create a more supple multinational airmobile division and which will be a fore-runner in its rapid reaction force capacities. With the 4th airmobile division, France makes use of a particularly flexible tool whose tactics are ceaselessly being brought up to date. It is quite evident that airmobile combat has an interesting future.

Without going into detail, a helicopter assault can be described as follows: 1; decision. 2; observation and selection of landing zone by use of satellite photos and aerial reconnaissance. 3; tactical reconnaissance by observation helicopters

The vegetation is different but this Bell helicopter assault by the US Vth Corps in Germany is reminiscent of the grand moments of the "CAV" in Vietnam twenty-five years earlier.

and commando teams. 4; bombardment of landing zones and their immediate vicinity by aircraft and artillery. 5; suppression of AA defences by aviation and attack helicopters. 6; assault helicopter and attack helicopter escort, the first wave of infantrymen is transported by helicopter. 7; second wave of infantry landed near the target. 8; third wave bringing support fire. 9; fourth wave is logistic bringing fuel and ammunition. 10; helicopter transport of the artillery.

Soldiers are in general transported by Huey, Puma, Mi-8/17 or BlackHawk, and the heavier helicopters, such as Chinook or CH-53, deal with reinforcements, ammunition and artillery.

Above: A typical helicopter assault: a storm of dust, roaring rotors, whirring blades as the crack corps leaps from the cabin. Here Italian paras from the Folgore with an AB-205.

In East Europe the MI-8/17 is the principal helicopter. Here a Hungarian machine on the terrain at Solznoc.

79

SIKORSKY S-58/H-34 CHOCTAW

Nowadays, several first generation helicopters are still flying with new engines and a modern avionic. This is the case with the S-58 initially developed for the US Navy as an anti-submarine heli-copter and which flew for the first time in 1954. This model was adopted by the US Army under the name H-34 Choctaw. Because of its capacity to transport 18 infantrymen it saw action in Vietnam and Israel and served in a number of NATO and allied countries in the sixties. The H-34 Choctaw is no longer on the market, there are only 150 machines with new engines and which are destined essentially for the civil market. Nevertheless 12 S-58T were delivered to the Royal Thai Air Force where they will serve within its squadron 201 based at Lop Buri.

Indonesia also has 12 models and Argentina uses three S-58 in the presidential fleet.

A modernised Sikorsky S-54 from squadron N°75 of the Royal Thai Air Force leaves the Special Forces school at Lop bury for a parachute jump.

Characteristics

Rotor diameter: 17.07m
Length: 17.27m
Engine: Pratt and Whitney PT 6T T 1800hp
Empty weight: 3515kg, with full load: 5897 kg
Maximum speed: 196 km/h, cruising: 156 km/h
Range: 397km.

The British still use about sixty Westland Wessex, a Rolls-Royce turbine version of the S-58. Here a machine from 60 squadron of the RAF seen during exercise COLD GROUSE 95.

SIKORSKY S-61 SEA KING

Malaysia is one of the only countries to use the S-61 Sea King as a ground attack helicopter. Known locally as "NURI" they often operate above the jungle.

Characteristics

Rotor diameter: 18.90 m
Turning rotor length: 22.15 m
Length of fuselage: 17.02 m
Engines: Two Rolls-Royce
Gnome H-1400
1T turbines each
developing 1660 hp.
Empty weight: 5620 kg
Weight with full load: 9752 kg
Internal Fuel capacity: 3741 l
with extra internal tank + 863 l
Maximum speed: 226 km/h
Cruising speed: 204 km/h
Maximum autonomy: 1742 km

A naval helicopter, therefore not really a subject of this book, the Sea King MK-2, an anti-submarine craft, has nonetheless given rise to a troop transport version, the Westland Commando, which equips the ground forces of Qatar and Egypt. The craft has the same engine, and is only differentiated from the outside by an absence of the radom and AS equipment. The large cabin capacity means that 28 equipped soldiers or a load of 3402 kg can be carried. Saudi Arabia made an order of 24 Westland Commando which were then sold to Egypt.

Egypt also acquired four extra craft modified to carry out counter-electronic operations.

The other large operator of the Westland Commando is the Emirate of Qatar which has twelve. Some of them are armed with 12.7 mm machine gun pods, SURA rockets and even Exocet missiles. Malaysia uses 30 S-61 A (the US version of the Sea King) under the name of "Nuri" and modified for troop transport.

The Westland Commando HC-MK-4 is in service in Egypt and Qatar. Here a Qatari machine at Doha airport.

BELL MODEL 204/UH-1
MODEL UH-1D/H IROQUOIS

The Huey was immortalised during Vietnam where it was the "all-purpose machine". Francis Ford Coppola's film "Apocalypse Now" made it a legend. The Huey is as important in the history of helicopters as the Spitfire or the Mustang are to the history of planes. The "doug, doug, doug" of its two-blade rotor will remain forever etched in the memory of the dozens of wounded soldiers anxiously awaiting evacuation, soldiers short of ammunition or simply those in an isolated area happy to receive some post or a few beers. However, the history of this most versatile helicopter begins rather modestly. In 1950 the US Army launched a programme for a simple machine destined to evacuate medical personnel and also for low visibility training. Thanks to Prof. Aselm Franz and his German team (this was after the war), the Bell Helicopter Company took the risk of mounting one XT-53 750hp turbine on its airframe only, which was at that time a real revolution. That was how the three prototypes, named Model 204 or XH-40 were built. The first flew in 1956 and the US Army, which were enthusiastic about it,

thus adopted its first craft propelled by one turbine. Production was launched in 1959 and the craft, as well as its official name of UH-1A Iroquois rapidly gained its immortal nickname of "Huey" (Helicopter Utility 1).

After the first version was improved, the UH-1B, manufactured from March 1961, made use of more powerful T-53-L-5 960hp engines then L-11 1100hp which allowed a considerable increase in the weight and the utility load. This version interested Japan which assembled 89 craft at the Fuji plant as well as Italy which acquired the manufacturing license under the name of Agusta Bell AB 204 and resold it in a number of countries. The US Army had 2500 craft and this success encouraged Bell to improve the performance of its machine by launching the UH-1D version which kept the same T-53-L-11 Lycoming engine with a new rotor of 14.65m in diameter. The cabin was lengthened by approximately 50%, thus allowing the transport of eight infantrymen or six wounded with a nurse and also two pilots. The load carried reached 2270kg for a total mass of 4309kg. The introduction of a new TA-5313A 1400hp engi-

Shining under the winter sun in the Bavarian Alps, this German Bell UH-1D takes part in an exercise with the Gebirgsjäger (mountain troops).

With its rounded nose, two-blade rotor and an inimitable noise, the M-60 with its "door gunner". The myth of the "Huey" captured in one picture. Here a craft of the 101st Air Assault in the gulf.

ne transformed the UH-ID model into the UH-IH, the definitive version of this craft. With the escalation of the Vietnam war, Bell built up to two machines a day and the US Army acquired 2008 UH-IH which will remain in service until the 21st century. The production of the UH-IH was completed with an order of 40 craft for Turkey in 1986. Dornier in Germany also built 352 UH-ID under license which became the medium standard helicopter of the Bundeswehr where as the Taiwanese firm AIDC produced 118 UH-IH for the Chinese nationalist army. Agusta-Bell built more than 100 which served in many armed forces in the world. Widely exported to US allies, and very reliable in combat, the immortal Huey is proof of military technology and a prominent figure in the military history of the end of the twentieth century.

Characteristics

For model UH-1H

Rotor diameter: 14.65m
Length: 17.62m
Engine: One Textron Lycoming T-53-L-13 turbine developing 1400hp.
Empty weight: 2363kg.
Weight with full load: 4309kg.
Troop transport weight: 4100kg
Fuel capacity 844 l, 1935 l with two auxiliary tanks.
Cruising speed: 204 km/h
Autonomy: 511 km.

BELL MODEL 204/UH-1 MODEL UH-1D/H IROQUOIS

From the poles to the jungle,
from the desert to the paddy-field,
the Huey is omnipresent as this series of photos shows.

Norway

Turkey

Italy

Greece

Spain

Brazil

Singapore

Honduras

Taiwan

Japan

Philippines

Singapore

US and German

85

BELL MODEL 212

In 1968, negotiations between Bell helicopter, the Canadian government and Pratt & Whitney Canada brought about an Iroquois twin-turbine development programme. The engine selected was the PT-6-T Turbo Twin-Pac, consisting of two turbines mounted side by side but the craft was able to fly on a single turbine creating 900hp. With this model, able to carry almost 1 tonne more than the first Huey, Bell became part of the history of aeronautics as the mass of the machine had been multiplied by 2.15, from the appearance of the first prototype, which was unique. The adaptation of the Turbo Twin-Pac did not pose any particular problem and the new model was called Bell model 212. The military designation was UH-1N and the US Army acquired 79 models which were used mainly in the Special Forces. Because of its two engines, it is more reliable over the sea than a single engine. The UH-1N was above all a machine destined for the US Navy and the Marine corps but this naval use is not covered in this book. The Canadian armed forces acquired 50 models under the name CUH-1N which were rapidly transformed into CH-135 "Twin Huey". As was the case for the model UH-1B and H, the Italian firm Agusta acquired a license for manufacture and sold it under the name AB-212. It was mainly in its anti-submarine version that the AB-212 had its success as an export item. Several countries nonetheless use it for terrestrial operations.

An AB-212 of the Hubschrauber Geschwader I with its rotor turning, in a village in the Tyrol during exercise WINTERSTURM 89.

With its very becoming camouflage in two shades of green, this AB-212 takes off from Viterbo, the large training base of the Italian Air Corps. The nozzles of the "Twin Pac" turbines characteristic of this model are easily distinguishable.

Under the Arabian sun, a Saudi AB-212 waits for a mission. The camouflage is well-adapted to the desert.

Characteristics

Rotor diameter: 14.69m
Length: 17.46m
Engines: Two Pratt & Whitney Canada T 400 CP, 1800hp.
Empty weight: 2787kg
Weight with full load: 5080kg
Fuel capacity: 814 l,
with internal supplementary tank 1814 l,
or 2268 l with external supplementary tank.
Maximum speed: 259 km/h
Cruising speed: 230 km/h
Mission range: 420 km.

A flight in formation for these Bell 212 of squadron 31 of the Bangladesh Air Force.
The curtains visible in the windows of the nearest craft indicate a VIP transport version.

BELL MODEL 412 AND AB-412 "GRIFONE"

The large four-blade rotor immediately identifies the "412". Here a machine of the ALE equipped with a large rocket launcher seen during exercise FARFADET, in the south of France.

Characteristics

Rotor diameter: 14.02 m
Turning rotor length: 17.07 m
Length of fuselage: 12.92 m
Engines: Pratt & Whitney Canada PT-6T-3B
1 Turbo Twin Pac developing 1400 hp
Empty weight: 2935 kg - Weight with full load: 5397 kg
Fuel capacity: 1249 l plus an internal
supplementary tank of 621 l
Autonomy: 695 km - Maximum speed: 259 km
Cruising speed: 230 km/h

The youngest in a long line of Huey, the 412 model is a powerful machine whose origins lay in the continuing improvement in the performance of the model 212. In spite of these qualities the 212 had a speed of only 185 kmph over the sea and a mission radius limited to 420 km. The project of Bell was to increase these performances without changing the airframe which was completely satisfactory. A slightly more powerful motorisation and tanks carrying 1249 litres instead of 814 improved the autonomy a little, but it was principally the new four blade rotor in composite material which differentiated the model 412 from its illustrious predecessors. The first two prototypes flew in 1979 and the Bell company is still producing the craft today. The centre of production has been transferred to Quebec, although a number of components are still manufactured at Fort Worth, USA. The airframe has, of course, undergone numerous improvements such as the Bell 412SP, 100 models of which, under the name CH-46 Griffon, were ordered by Canada. The craft is built under license in Indonesia and following its tradition of co-operation with Bell, Agusta produced an AB-412 Grifone. The Italian AB-412 are powerfully armed with machine guns, door-mounted guns and rocket-launchers. The Grifone can carry 14 equipped infantrymen.

This Bell-412 SP of squadron 339 refuels near Trömso. Note the camouflage, the low visibility roundel and the plates fixed at the rear of the landing gear designed to stop the craft from sinking into the snow.

NORWEGIAN ROYAL AIR FORCE

The northernmost, and one of the least populated countries in Europe, Norway has nonetheless a vital strategic importance as it controls the access to the sea of the Russian fleet based in Murmansk. Norway does not have a light aviation wing of the army, its helicopter units are attached to the Kongelige Norske Luftforsvaret or Royal Norwegian Air Force. At the end of the 80's the Bell UH-1B gave up its place to the superb Bell 412 SP which were modified to be able to operate in the arctic. Two squadrons operated with this type of machine and we can also mention the existence of a reserve unit using a number of machines operating on oil platforms in the North sea. Four Bell 412 SP are doing admirable work on behalf of UNPROFOR from Tuzla in Bosnia.

Battle order:

339 squadron: Bell 412 SP (Barduloss)
720 squadron: Bell 412 SP (Rygge)
756 squadron: various (Rygge)

Stock: 18 Bell 412 SP.

More than 300 km north of the arctic circle a Bell-412 SP takes off in a whirlwind of snow. The craft belongs to squadron 339 engaged in a NATO exercise.

This small civilian Fennec is a reservist of squadron 756 sent from its oil platform for a NATO exercise. The Norwegian roundel is stylised on the tail beam.

NEUTRAL EUROPEAN COUNTRIES

Austria

An alpine country and the crossroads of central Europe, Austria has a relatively high number of transport and liaison helicopters including AB-205, AB-212, OH-58 and several Alouette III. These machines are attached to the aviation division of the Austrian army. Austria does not have its own air force.

Battle order:

Hubschraubergergeschwader 1
1st Staffel: AB-212 (Tull-Langenlebarn)
2nd Staffel: AB-206 (Tull-Langenlebarn)
3rd Staffel: OH-58B (Tull-Langenlebarn)

Hubschraubergergeschwader 2
1st Staffel: Alouette III (Aigen im Enstal)
2nd Staffel: Alouette III (Aigen im Enstal)

Hubschraubergergeschwader 3
1st Staffel: AB-212 (Linz-Hörsching)
2nd Staffel: AB-204 B (Linz-Hörsching)

Stock: 21 AB-204B, 10 AB-206 A, 23 AB-212, 11 Bell OH-58B, 26 Alouette III.

AB-212 of the Hubschrauberger geschwader 1.

Sweden

In order to keep its neutrality Sweden, which has a considerable maritime presence in the Baltic sea, has always consented to heavy financial sacrifices for its defence. As for fixed wing aircraft, there are many models of national construction, but the Arméflygkar is comprised of AB-204 and AB-412 for transport, Jet Ranger for observation and BO-105 equipped with the anti-tank HeliTow system. The craft have a common name. The Cougars used in SAR can be attached to the air force and also be used for transport of troops such as the Kawasaki Vertol KV-107 (Hkp-4) of the Navy.

Battle order:

1st company of helicopter transport Hkp-6A
2nd company of helicopter transport Hkp-3C
3rd company of helicopter transport Hkp-9A
Training unit (Skolavdelning) Kkp-3 and Hkp-6A.

The light aviation school uses all existing models. Each sector of aerial defence, and there are five spread over the country, uses one section SAR on Hkp-10 Cougar.

Stock: 10 AS-532 UL Cougar (Hkp-10), 16 AB-204 B (Hkp-3), 19 AB-206 A (Hkp-6). 5 AB-412 plus 12 on option, 20 MBB - BO-105 CB (Hkp-9), 26 Hughes 300 C (Hkp-5).

A Swedish Hkp-9 alias BO-105 decorated with two polar bears.

Switzerland

This alpine country has built itself a solid reputation concerning its armed forces which are almost entirely made up of a reserve force who have carried out a number of calls to arms during their existence. This system also applies to the aeroplanes of the air force which is in fact the Vth Corps of the Swiss army. The helicopter

Battle order:

4 aviation regiment - Fliegerregiment 4
1 squadron: Alouette III and Cougar
5 squadron: Alouette III and Cougar
6 squadron: Alouette III and Cougar
8 squadron: Alouette III and Cougar
plus a Super Puma VIP at 35 Flieger at Zurich.

Stock: 15 Aérospatiale AS-532 UL Cougar and 71 SA-316 Alouette III.

A Swiss Alouette III equipped with special landing gear for icy conditions.

pilots are of course reservists often belonging to Swissair and who know their terrain perfectly. The helicopters, essentially Cougar and Alouette III are attached to 4 aviation regiment

Finland

This Nordic country is considered as one of the bravest since its war with the Soviet Union in the winter of 1939. It has a small number of helicopters amalgamated with the air force or Ilmavoimat.

Battle order:

Laponie communication squadron, (Yhteslentue) on Mi-8.
Transport squadron (Kuljettusientoläivue) on Mi-8.
Army communication squadron on Hughes 500 D.

Stock: 7 Mi-8 "HIP" and 2 Hughes 500 D.

A Finnish MI-8 seen in Lapland during exercise Tuisku.

Ireland

The Irish Air corps or Aer-Chor na-h Eireann uses several helicopters of French construction.

Battle order:

No. 3 squadron: Alouette II and Dauphin 2 at Finner camp.
Helicopter school on Gazelle.

Stock: 2 SA-342 Gazelle, 5 Dauphin 2 SAR, 8 SA-316 Alouette III.

A Swiss Cougar of 4 aviation regiment.

The helicopter made its entrance in conventional war in Europe (1) when a Yugoslavian army Gazelle was attacked by the Slovenians above Ljublijama in June 1991. With a clear superiority at the beginning of the conflict, the Serbs used their Mi-8 on a small scale, notably to try to control the border posts between Slovenia and Austria and, later, in certain regions of Bosnia. The Gazelles made under license at Mostar, were however, massively used in the corridor battle in 1992, and a black Gazelle expertly piloted caused numerous losses to the Vth corps of the Bosnian army at Bihac. After the war the Mi-8 and Gazelle were used mainly for MEDEVAC and resupplying of troops in each camp... losses were incurred by several Croat and Bosnian Mi-8's used for resupplying Bosnian enclaves with ammunition. During these operations several helicopters were even painted white, the UN colour, so as to confuse the NATO aircraft which had the responsibility of enforcing the no-fly zone over Bosnia.

In less than three years, Croatia succeeded in creating a respectable, small air force, whose helicopter section was made up of Mi-8, Mi-17, Mi-24 and several Hughes 500. It played its part very successfully in the gaining back of lost territories. Bosnia used Mi-8's. The UN forces used helicopters from their arrival at the end of 1991, and an Italian Bell 205 at the disposal of the European community was destroyed by a Serbian Mig-21 causing the deaths of 8 observers. A French DETA-

A Croatian Mi-8 at Split airport. These craft, certainly of Slovak origin, are used on all fronts.

THE BALKAN WAR

LAT of Puma and Gazelle was based at Split in company with British Lynx to support operations in Bosnia, whereas 4 Norwegian Bell 412 operated from Tuzla. Several Mi-17's and two enormous Ukrainian Mi-26's acted as a shuttle between Split and Zagreb. The white of the UN did not particularly protect these machines which were often captured by belligerents and it was a real miracle that no UN helicopter was downed.

Following the taking of hostages, in May '95, the attitude of the west hardened, and resulted in a multinational rapid reaction force being sent with an Anglo-French helicopter contingent of 8 Gazelle and 7 Puma for ALAT, 18 Lynx and 9 Gazelle for the Army Air corps and 6 Puma and 6 Chinook for the RAF.

The following list gives only a very rough estimate of helicopters used by the fighting factions due to the secretive nature of war.

Yugoslavia (Serbia Montenegro). This country, which was not directly involved in the conflict, used 10 squadrons of helicopters divided between 40 Mi-8 and 120 Soko Gazelle Partizan.

Serbian Republic of Bosnia: several Gazelle and Mi-8 divided between two squadrons.

Croatia: Approximately ten Hind Mi-24, fifteen or so Mi-8/17 and several Hughes 500.

Bosnia: Approximately ten Mi-8.

Slovenia has just formed a small air force with Gazelle Partizan, 2 AB-206, 7 Bell 412 and an A-109 Hirundo attached to the 15th Aviation Brigade whilst Macedonia uses several Mi-8.

Left, near Ploce two Gazelle protect a Puma of the 5th RHC.
This unit was sent to give support to the western rapid reaction force.

Photos opposite from top:
A Puma from DETALAT has just put down some
Canadian soldiers at Visoko. A shell could fall at any time.

French DETALAT Gazelle at Split.

Norwegian Bell-412 at Tuzla used for a MEDEVAC.

British Lynx MK-7 at Split.

(1) Helicopters of the British armed forces have of course been used against the IRA.

SA-330 - PUMA (AEROSPATIALE)

From Chad to the Gulf and from Rwanda to Yugoslavia, the Puma is the workhorse of the French Army and of many other armed forces which have used it intensively in combat and have appreciated both its reliability and its robustness. The Puma represents an ini-

This Puma from the 5th RHC, which has just taken some paras on board during IBERIA 91, has a superb FAR camouflage.

tial and very fortunate development of a medium helicopter destined to replace the S-58 Sikorsky used in Algeria. The RAF was also interested in this "all weather" helicopter project ion order to replace its Whirlwinds and Belvedere. As a result of this the Puma was included in the famous Anglo-French helicopter agreement. Westland built 292 Gazelle and 48 Puma and the French navy bought 40 Lynx. Eight SA-330 prototypes were ordered in June 1963 and the first flew at Marignane on 15 April 1965. The last of these prototypes were evaluated in England. The first 40 models ordered by the RAF under the name Puma HC-MK1 were delivered in November 1970. The two 1320hp Turbomeca Turbo turbines gave the Puma the ability to lift its own weight and a considerable load, together reaching 6400kg, with a speed of 280km/h for the first versions. The initial production included the 125 SA-330B models ordered by ALAT, the SA-330C destined for export and PumaHC-MK1 of the RAF. 37 machines of a more powerful version, the SA-330H and G were ordered by the French air force for SAR missions. New rotors in glass fibre transformed some of the SA-330J and H into SA-330 J and L. 40% of ALAT craft were modernised in this way as well as some Puma of the RAF. 686 Puma were produced in France.

In the Weser valley two Puma from 230 squadron (Tiger) RAF are working for the 24th airmobile brigade.

The Rumanian firm IAR obtained a manufacturing license for the SA-330L in 1977 and 200 craft were built including several for France. The French and British versions can carry machine guns and 20mm side guns firing via the side door, the Rumanian Puma are equipped for pylon ground support for 4 AYT-3 Sagger missile rocket pods and machine gun pods. The Puma was also built under license by ATLAS in South Africa.

Some of these later versions of the Puma have a modified nose in order to carry an Omega ORB-31 radar and some "flotation bags" like some of the 10 Puma delivered to Portugal. Indonesia had some assembly kits for 11 SA-330J in 1983.

Nowadays the French and British Puma have little to do with the first versions, except for the silhouette. The craft are filled with "black boxes" and flare launchers. The Puma of the RAF are especially well modernised with new filters, an ARI. 18228 radar warning and a dashboard adapted to night flying goggles. In 1991, for the Gulf war, British Puma were equipped with M-130 flare launchers and AN/AAR-47 missile warning system. An AN/ALQ-144 scrambler designed to throw off course possible IR `missiles fired by the IRA was installed in craft operating in Northern Ireland. Some even had night surveillance equipment for special missions under the name of Pleasant 3. In France, the Puma was chosen as the future surveillance helicopter of the ALAT battlefield with the mounting of the ORCHID/HORIZON radar.

This Argentinean Puma surveys the pampas. Apart from one coast guard craft, Argentinean Pumas were not engaged in the Falklands.

A South African Puma at Oshikati in Namibia getting ready for take-off for a mission in Angola.

PORTUGAL

D uring their "colonial" war in Africa, the Portuguese gained a unique experience during airmobile operations directed against Marxist guerrillas.

Nowadays, helicopters make up part of the Força Aérea Portuguesa but with the creation of a rapid reaction brigade and the possible purchase of Bell UH-IH and Cobra, an ALAT will be created, and almost certainly based at Tancos.

Battle order:

Esquadra de transporte Tactico 552 on Alouette III.
Esquadra de Busqua e Salvamento 503 and 504 on Puma.
Esquadra de Instruçao 111 on Alouette III.

Stock: 10 SA-330C and SA-330 Puma, 14 SA-316 B & C Alouette III.

A Portuguese Puma flying over the Tagus estuary.

L'ALAT: ARMY LIGHT

Just as for standard aircraft at the turn of the century, the French were pioneers of helicopters... It took place during the fifties, in Algeria, at the time when the Pentagon challenged the massive use of helicopters. Large formations of Sikorsky supported by fragile Alouette II, some of which were armed, scoured the N. African mountains looking for fellaghas. It was from these flying units, which held the spirit of soldiering dear, that the ALAT was born in 1955. Nowadays the same spirit of humility linked to a true professionalism motivates these pilots. However, ALAT is an exceptional combat tool and its domestically constructed helicopters are capable of striking hard and far, return for resupplying and then to strike again. Because of an error concerning the armour on the light Gazelle, the ALAT Chiefs of Staff constructed a whole doctrine of combat based on mobility, speed of action and dissimulation. As opposed to the Germans, British and to a lesser extent the Americans (1) whose helicopters fight with their armour on the level of an army corps, the 4th DAM was conceived to strike the enemy right wherever it is situated. Invented to "break" the tank, the airmobile division is capable of going more than 250km, of firing a salvo of 360 antitank missiles, of resupplying deep within the battlefield and of doing 250km in another direction to

release a new load of missiles. During exercise "Kecker Spatz" which took place in Germany in 1988, the leading parts of a panzerdivision were "eliminated" by attacking Gazelle, without having seen a single one. Endless missions in Africa, the Balkans and the participation of ALAT in the Gulf war also taught the French pilots not to concentrate solely on the central Europe theatre of operation for which the 4th DAM had been conceived. In the Gulf, where there were no minarets to hide behind, tactics had to be reviewed but ALAT, adjustable wherever necessary, is capable of facing up to many unplanned situations. As they were using a tool of intervention and political "gesticulation", ALAT pilots encountered sparks in Chad and in the Gulf. These maritime transfer exercises are carried out once a year during DAMTAM exercised where a simulation of a Mediterranean takes place using the Foch or Clemenceau aircraft carriers as a resupply base. ALAT has two major parts: combat ALAT with the 4th DAM and 3rd BAM (Airmobile Brigade) and territorial ALAT equipped with light machines destined for liaison and assistance to the command. The mixed base unit is the RHC (Combat Helicopter Regiment) which generally includes an EHR (Helicopter Reconnaissance Squadron), an EHAP (Protection Support Helicopter Squadron) on Gazelle

A large assembly of machines from the 3rd RHC during an ALAT presentation to foreign military attaches at Canjuers.

AIRCRAFT

20mm, three EHA (Attack Helicopter Squadrons) on Gazelle HOT and one EHM (Manœuvre Helicopter Squadron) on Puma.

Transport and attack missions are done by the RHCM (Regiment of command and Manœuvre Helicopters) composed of 4 squadrons of 11 Puma or Cougar and one command squadron on Gazelle. Lastly, let us mention the 6th RHCM which is comprised of two antitank squadrons, a protections support squadron, a Mistral squadron (AA) and two Puma squadrons.

With the arrival of the Tiger, near 200, ALAT will pass from a single arm craft of the single armament generation to a revolutionary machine, perfected and equipped with several armament systems, which will doubtless bring about with it a total restructuring of the doctrine and also the squadrons themselves. As for the Puma, its replacement by the NH-90 will depend on the availability of funds.

(1) Except for the 101st Air Assault Division.

__These photos show us the main types of ALAT helicopters:__

__Right from top to bottom: Alouette III of the 1st GHL, Gazelle canon of the 5th RHC, Puma of the 1st RHC, Cougar of the 4th RHCM.__

Gazelle HOT of the 3rd RHC.

ALAT

Battle order:

3rd BAM (Aeromobile Brigade) with the 6th RHCM (Compiegne) and the 7th RHC (Essey-les-Nancy).
4th DAM (Division Aeromobile)
with the 1st RHC (Phalsbourg), the 3rd RHC (Etain), the 5th RHC (Pau) and the 4th RHCM (Nancy).
Territorial ALAT regroups the GHL (Light Helicopter Group) made up of: 1st GHL (Bordeaux),
5th GHL (Lyon),

6th GHL (Metz), also including the COMALAT at Villacoublay, the HQ squadron at Mureaux and
the French forces squadron in Germany at Baden-Baden. These small formations use Alouette II/III
and Gazelle.
Four squadron schools are based at Cannet des Maures and also at Dax for mountain flying.
Three DETALAT made up of
five Puma at Djibouti,
Ndjamena (Chad) and Bangui (Central African Republic).

Stock: 4 AS-555 Fennec, 157 SA-341 Gazelle, 187 SA-342 Gazelle, 134 SA 330 Puma, 24 SA 532 UL Cougar, 134 Sud SE Alouette II, 64 Sud SA Alouette III.

A squadron of Gazelle HOT, their missiles unmounted, take off from the Clemenceau, during a DAMTAM exercise.
Using the aircraft carriers as a refuelling platform an RHC can cross the Mediterranean.

The desert sand has scratched the paint of this Puma of the RHC engaged in operation Daguet. Note the three white stripes of the coalition.

Three Cougar of the 4th RHCM leave the terrain at Perpignan during exercise FARFADET. Note the three-shade central Europe camouflage. Cougars were also engaged in Kurdistan.

AS-532 COUGAR AS-332 (AEROSPATIALE)

The success of the Puma led its constructor to develop an improved version; the AS-332 was born. The general outline was the same with the exception of a large radome under the tail beam and a nose radome containing a Bendix/King RDR 1400 or Honeywell Primus 500 weather radar.

The undercarriage can be retracted and the Super Puma rotor relies heavily on the technology of glass fibre. Even though it was initially destined for the civil market, the Super Puma, renamed Cougar, was only of interest to the military because of several revolutionary elements in its design. The gearbox is, for example, capable of functioning for a whole hour without lubricant and the rotor remains operational 40 hours after being hit by a 12.7mm projectile. The machine is powered by a pair of Makila 1A turbines each delivering 1780hp and not requiring any reheating, which means the Super Puma can take off very rapidly. The first flight took place 13 September 1978 and the standard Super Puma was ready in 1981 under the name AS-332 B. In January 1990, the military versions were rechristened Cougar AS-532 and gave rise to diffe-

rent variations: AS-532 AC and UC for short fuselage machines, armed or not, AS-532 AL or UL for long fuselage versions, armed or not, AS 532 MC and SC for naval versions. After having been tested on the Puma, the HORIZON battlefield surveillance radar was mounted on the Cougar. Tested over 24 missions during the Gulf war, the HORIZON radar was to be mounted on six AS-532 UL HORIZON destined for ALAT. Thirty AS-532 Cougar have also been put into operation by ALAT within the 4th RHCM at Nancy since 1991. As for the Puma, the Indonesian firm IPTN has acquired a manufacturing license and produces its own machines. The Cougar was also to become one of the principal combat helicopters of the Turkish army with an order of 50 models, many of which were constructed in Turkey. The Netherlands has chosen the Cougar as a medium helicopter for their new airmobile brigade representing another recent commercial success.

The Cougar is a worthy substitute for the Puma; 400 models have been ordered, a good proportion of those for military use.

A Cougar of the 4th RHCM flies over the vines of the South West of France during exercise FARFADET 92.
Craft embarked on the Foudre and the Orage took part in landing operations.

*A Cougar of the FAMET
has just transported
some Spanish soldiers
from the 5th airmobile division
near Almeria. If the BlackHawk
is not selected, the Cougar
will be the principal
medium helicopter of FAMET.*

*Front view
of a Swiss Cougar
on manœuvres
in the Swiss Jura.
The craft is attached
to the 4th Swiss aviation regiment.*

Characteristics

For the
AS-532 UC Cougar version.
Rotor diameter: 15.60m
Length turning rotor: 18.70m
Fuselage: 15.53m
Engines: Two Turbomeca Makila
1A1 developing 1877 hp
Empty weight: 4330kg
Weight with full load: 9350kg
Internal fuel capacity: 1497l plus a
possible 1900l in spare tank
Maximum speed 278 km/h
Cruising speed: 262 km/h
Mission radius:
618 km with a time of 3 h 20 mn.

TURK KARA HAVACILIGI

As it is surrounded by countries which are not very friendly, Turkey has had to devote itself to maintaining a sizable helicopter force regrouped within the Türc Kara Havaciligi or Army air corps. The helicopter is of course particularly well-adapted to operations over the mountainous terrain found in the centre and east of the country and the Cobra has been used a lot in the fight against Kurdish guerrillas of the PKK, and especially at night. Along with those of Israel and the US, the Turkish Cobras are the only ones to be equipped with NTS (Night Targeting System), thus allowing night operations to take place. The Turkish army air corps is undergoing a modernisation programme and its stock consists of about 260 machines. Each army has an aviation regiment (Hava Alayi) composed of three aviation battalions (Hava Taburu) with about thirty machines some of which are light aircraft.

The 1st Hava Alayi based in Istanbul operates for the 1st Army in the north-west of the country.

The 2nd, at Maltaya, put its machines into operation for the 2nd army in central and southern Turkey whereas the 3rd Hava Alayi based at Erzican supports units of the 3rd Army in the east of the country. An "Aegean" Hava Alayi covers operations of the Aegean army based at Izmir.

Basic training is carried out within the Army light aviation school based at Güvercinlik which has four battalions: elementary training, observation, liaison, attack and transport. The units of the school are sometimes used in a real operation such as operation Steel in Iraqi Kurdistan.

The current stocklist is as follows: for transport and assault missions Turkey has 14 AB-204s, 64 AB-205s, 2 AB-212s, 96 UH-1Hs, and 50 S-70 BlackHawk and 20 Cougar built under license and which were operational in 1995. Thirty extra Cougars should have been ordered. For attack, the Army air corps uses 28 AH-1P and 14 AH-1W and would like to bring the total of these attack helicopters to 140. For observation, Turkey only uses three OH-58A which were to be supported from 1995 by 20 AB-206 B. The Turks are also interested in purchasing the Kiowa warrior OH-58D. Basic training is done with 26 H-269C and 9 R-22.

The army hopes to find the financial resources to purchase a certain number of Chinooks. Lastly there is the Jandarma, a paramilitary force which takes part in anti-guerilla operations and which uses 4 Pumas, 19 Mi-17 and 6 S-70.

Two Turkish Cobra AH-1F taking-off from Güvercinlik for a training flight.

ELLINIKI AEROPORIA STRATOU

A Greek Huey from the 1st TEAS is winching up some oil barrels.

In case of any conflict in the Aegean, the helicopter would be essential to the Greek armed forces for resupplying the many islands or to reinforce them with new troops. On the northern border, Macedonia and Albania, the mountainous terrain favours the use of the helicopter; the only way of outflanking enemy defensive positions. Created in 1956, the Elliniki Aerporia Stratou (Army Air Corps) is made up of three Tagmas (battalions) and one school. The 1st Tagma Elliniki Aeroporia Stratous (TEAS) is based in the centre of the country at Stefanoviklio near Larissa and is comprised of three companies (lokos) of medium helicopter AB-205, AB-206 and UH-1H.

The second TEAS, situated at Megara, a suburb of Athens, is the largest. It is made up of four lokos of medium helicopters UH-1H, AB-205 and 206 and a company of heavy helicopters with the CH-47. The third TEAS is at Alexandroupolis in the north of Greece and is comprised of three lokos of medium helicopters. The school is at Stefanoviklio and has four lokos, two of which are fixed wing, on one the small Hughes NH-300 and one on UH-1H for proficiency. The current stock is 60 UH-1H, 50 AB-205 A for medium transport and attack, 10 CH-47 C Chinook for heavy transport, 16 AB-206 for observation and 30 NH-C for training. After 150 flying hours on the latter model, Greek trainee pilots move on to the Huey simulator at Stefanoviklio before going on to Jet Ranger and UH-1H.

All Greek helicopters can be armed with machine guns or miniguns but the arrival of 20 AH-64D in 1995 considerably increased the fire power of the Elliniki Aeroporia Stratou.

Cyprus

This island is one of the most heavily militarised in the world and the Greek national Guard has a small number of helicopters; 4 Gazelle HOT, 2 Bell 206 Jet Ranger, which can be equipped with rockets, and 3 Mi-2s. On the Turkish side of the island there are Alouette III and Bell UH-1H, doubtless coming from the Turkish army.

The crew of a Super Cobra prepares for a mission.
The flying equipment is American.

MI-8/17 HIP-C AND HIP-H

In October 1973 the Egyptians and Syrians opened the Kippur war by a daring series of helicopter raids, one of which gave Mount Hermont to the soldiers of Damas. The main military tool of these operations was the Soviet Mi-8 helicopter named HIP by NATO. This ultra robust machine means as much to the Russians as the Huey does to the Americans. It is widely exported and has become one of the most widely used helicopters in the world. Its relatively cheap price makes it the "poor man's" helicopter and its simplicity makes it perfectly adapted to the third world where the maintenance of machines is uncertain. The story of the Mi-8 begins in 1960, when a new generation of Isotov turbines made their appearance. Much less bulky than those which were in the Mi-4 (standard helicopter of the Red Army), the Isotov turbines can be mounted above the cabin of a new machine although the tail beam and the Mi-4 rotors would be conserved. The fairly spacious cabin can hold 28 infantrymen. The first prototype (HIP-A) which flew in 1961, equipped with a single turbine, proved to be underpowered and was followed by a twin-turbine, the HIP-B, which had two Isotov TV-2. Mass production started with the Mi-8 HIP-C which also had taken up the rotor, although on a smaller scale, of the giant Mi-6. Two civilian versions, one being for VIP transport, were built, but it was principally the Mi-8T version which was to become known by soldiers the world over: semi-circular glass cockpit, and a curved small rear

Equipped with six "rocket pods", an Mi-17 from 129 squadron of the Indian air force is on standby at its base in Delhi. The MI-8 and 17 are the kingpin of Indian military transport.

With its red star, a Russian MI-8 recognisable by its straight tail rotor flies over the region of Raizan. This craft bears "Afghan" camouflage.

door make the Mi-8 a round helicopter. On each side of the fuselage, support pylons for UV-16-57 or UV-32-57 rocket launchers or light bombs can be mounted. Depending on their country of origin the Mi-8 can benefit from certain improvements; the Finns installed a weather radar under the nose and a headlight, the Egyptians put in British sand filters and the Angolans and Ethiopians placed Mi-17 PZU filters.

As for the Americans in Vietnam, the experience of combat in Afghanistan showed the necessity of using an armed escort helicopter for attack. This was the Mi-8 TB equipped with a 12.7mm chin machine gun with rocket pods and the possibility of firing Swatter antitank missiles. The Swatter was not designed for export, an export version, the Mi-TBK was proposed with six AT-3 Sagger and adopted by Germany, Nicaragua and Yugoslavia.

To improve the performance of the Mi-8 in tropical and mountainous areas, a new version capable of flying on a single engine was developed, the Mi-17 or HIP-H equipped with two Isotov TV-3-117 MT developing 1950hp. This version is immediately recognised by its tail rotor situated on the left. In the west this machine is known as the Mi-17 but the Russians call it the Mi-8 MT or Mi-8 TV according to the equipment being transported. Performance is considerably improved and consumption reduced.

The large cabin capacity as well as the reliability of the machine led the Russians to develop a number of specialised versions. The Mi-8PS HIP-D is a flying command post and radio centre recognisable by its extra aerials and a rectangular streamlining on the fuselage. It was replaced by the improved Mi-9 HIP G and destined for Soviet troops in Germany, also Czech, E. German and Hungarian troops.

The Mi-8 SMV HIP-J and Mi-8 PPA HIP-K are machines designed to jam radio communications. They are equipped with six large cross-shaped aerials at the rear of the fuselage. These same modifications are apparent on the Mi-17 PP named HIP-H (EW) by NATO.

Robust, simple and easy to maintain, the Mi-8/Mi-17 family of helicopters is just as content in the icy poles as in the desert, the jungles of the far east or the dust of the African savanna. This surely explains its well-deserved success.

A Czech MI-17 lands at Pilsen where a mixed combat (MI-17 and MI-24) helicopter regiment is stationed.

This Hungarian MI-8 is seen at Solznock where it is at the disposition of Magyardes special forces.

For the Mi-8 T HIP-C
Rotor diameter: 21.20m
Length of turning rotor: 25.24m
Length of fuselage: 18.17m
Engines: 2 Klimov (Isotov)TV2-117A
turbines, 1481hp each.
Empty weight: 7160kg
Weight with full load: 12000kg
Standard fuel capacity: 1870l
Exterior: 980l
Maximum speed: 250km/h
Maximum mission radius: 930km

A Croat MI-17 flies over the Dalmatian coast. The great number of machines available in the east meant a helicopter force could be formed fairly easily.

This Polish MI-8 is about to land paras of the 6th brigade. There is a side machine gun.

This photo, which would have been impossible to take a dozen or so years ago, shows us an MI-17 taking off from the strategic bomber base at Riazan. The three-shade camouflage is very effective.

The Sri-Lankan MI-17 are used intensively in anti-guerrilla operations. Here, two craft in formation.

EASTERN EUROPE

The old members of the Warsaw pact use mainly Russian helicopters, often built under license in the particular country. With the fall of the iron curtain, local industries are directing themselves towards producing national models or seeking to obtain licenses to manufacture Western models, like Rumania, which will construct the Cobra. Until then the majority of combat helicopter fleets will continue to be the indestructible Mi-8 and Mi-24 which, having lost their red stars, still have a long time ahead of them.

Poland

This country, which has produced several models of light helicopter, is beginning to create an aerial cavalry division. Therefore a light army aviation will soon be created but until then the helicopter fleet remains part of the Wojska Lotnicze or air force.

Apart from several liaison and transport machines, the majority of combat helicopters are attached to the 4th aviation corps.

*Two machines of Polish construction,
a Sokol and a Salamander of the 37th Pulk.*

Battle order:

36th Specjalny Pulk Lotnictawa transportowego (Varsovie) destined for VIP transport on Mi-8SP and Bell 412HP
The 2nd and 3rd Aerial Defence Corps each have at their disposal one escadra Lotnicza (liaison squadron) with the number of the corps on Mi-2.
The principal combat helicopter units are found in the 4th Aviation corps. These units are as follows:
17th eskadra Lotnicza on Mi-2 at Poznan.
37th Pulk Smiglowcow transportowych (assault) at Wielca on Mi-8/17
49th Pulk Smiglowcow Bojowych (combat) at Gdansk on Mi-24
56th Pulk Smiglowcow Bojowych (combat) at Latkowo on Mi-24
47th Szkolny Pulk Smiglowcow at Nowe Miasto on Mi-2 and Sokol.
First unit of the new airmobile division, the 37th Pulk, has just been attached to the military district at Cracovie and will be called the 251st Pulk Kawalerii Powiettrznej (PKP aerial cavalry regiment) with fifty helicopters divided into five squadrons.

Stock: 24 Mi-8, 3 Mi-8PD (PC Flying), 3 Mi-17, 14 Mi-24D and 16 Mi-24W HIND, 210 PZL Mi-2, 7 PZL W-3 Sokol, 5 PZL W-3WB "salamander" (plus an unknown number on order), 1 Bell 412 VIP.

Slovakia

The Velitelstvo Letecta a Protivdusnej Obrany Armady Slovenskej or air force and aerial defence of the Slovakian armed forces is made up of 115 aircraft and 25 helicopters.

Battle order:

2 squadron (Letka) of the 2nd regiment of transport on Mi-8/17 at Bratislava.
4th helicopter regiment (4 Vrtulnikovy Pluk) with 4 Letka (squadron) on Mi-24D,Mi-24W, Mi-17 and Mi-2.

Stock: 2 Mi-8 PPA (EW), 3 Mi-8 (VIP),27 Mi-17, 19 Mi-24 D/W, 18 PZL - Mi-2.

Czech republic

With the disintegration of Czechoslovakia, the existing stock of aircraft of Russian manufacture was divided: two thirds for the Czech republic and the remainder for Slovakia. Combat helicopters belong to the air force or Letectvo Protivzdusna Obrana Armady Ceske.

Battle order:

The 11th regiment of helicopters at Pilsen and Prostejov helicopter regiment depend on the 3rd aerial tactical corps regrouping both combat and transport helicopters.

Stock: 7 Mi-8, 32 Mi-17, 36 Mi-24D and W, 36 PZL MI-2.

A beautiful front view of an MI-24 Czech "Hind" from the 11th regiment at Pilsen.

Some Hungarian MI-24 of 1 squadron "Phoenix" at Szentkiraszabadja.

Rumania

This Latin country, unlike its neighbours who use exclusively Russian material, has begun manufacture under license of the Alouette III and the Puma by the firm IAR. Some of these craft fly in a configuration of the army. Rumanian industry has also just acquired the manufacturing license for the AH-1S Cobra, which will therefore become the first US combat machine used in service in East Europe.

Battle order:

It is difficult to have precise information concerning the battle order as Rumania is a very closed country. Nonetheless, we can confirm that there is a regiment of combat helicopters equipped with Mi-8/17 and IAR - 330 Puma at Bucharest-Otopeni and a regiment of antitank helicopters on Alouette III, IAR-316 and IAR-317 Airfox, Alouette equipped with Sagger missiles at Brasov. Several machines used for VIP transport are based at Bucharest.

Stock: 45 IAR-316B Alouette III, 12 IAR-317 Airfox are on order, 90 IAR-330L Puma, 20 Mi-8/17, 96 AH-IS Cobra (on order for 1999).

Hungary

This country has a small light army aviation, whose helicopter contingent is regrouped within the Bakony combat helicopter squadron and the mixed transport squadron at Szolnock. Most models in service are Russian.

Battle order:

Bakony Harcihelikopter Ezred based at Szentkiralszabadja
1 squadron "Phoenix" or 1 Harcihelikopter Szazad Fönix on Mi-24 D and V
2 squadron "Falcon" or 2 Harcihelikopter Szazad Kerescen on Mi-24D
3 squadron "Badger" or 3 Szallito Helikopter Szazad Borz on Mi-8TB
4 squadron mixed transport or 4 Szallito Helikopter Szazad Vegyes on Mi-8 TB, Mi-9 and Mi-17.
Mixed transport brigade at Szolnock
2 and 3 transport squadron or 2 and 3 Szallito Helikopter Szazad on Mi-8 T/S
4 and 5 liaison squadron or 4 and 5 Futarrepülo Helikopter Szazad on Mi-2
Germany has just completed delivery of 11 Mi-24 Hind which will form a new attack squadron where there will be a spare parts shop.

Stock: 35 Mi-8/17, b1 Mi-9 (flying PC),
5 Mi-17 P HIP-K (EW), 32 Mi-24D/W, 31 PZL-Mi-2.

A IAR-316 alias Alouette III of Rumania.

Bulgaria

The Bulgarian armed forces are in the process of reorganisation and have just created the 10th Aerial Tactical Corps (10 Corpus Taktichesa Aviatzia) which groups together all the helicopters in the country. There are two regiments: the 44th helicopter regiment (44 VAP Veroleten Aviopolk) based at Krumovo and which operates on Mi-8/17 and the 13th combat helicopter regiment or VBPV (Vertoleten Polk Boiny).

Stock: 7 Mi-8, 19, Mi-17, 44 Mi-24D and
V plus 12 in the process of being delivered, 18 PZL Mi-2.

A Bulgarian MI-8 from the 13th combat helicopter regiment.

RUSSIA

With Sikorsky and Piasecki, we can easily say that the modern helicopter was born in Russia, but as the two great scientists were chased out by the October revolution, they did not use their talents in the service of their country and the USSR stagnated in this area as a result. At the beginning of the sixties the few helicopters of the Red army in existence were copies of exis-

The completely new Kamov-50 "Hokum" is designed to replace the MIL MI-24 "HIND", as a combat helicopter.

ting American models, such as the Mi-4, which greatly resembled the Sikorsky S-55. Because of this, at the beginning of the seventies, the only area where NATO had a clear advantage over the Warsaw Pact in terms of both quality and quantity was in aeromobility. However, everything was to change within a few years with the introduction of the MI-8 "HIP" a reliable, all-purpose machine and above all the MI-24 Flying tank which had no real equivalent in the world when it first appeared and which was rapidly to become the bête noire of all NATO chiefs of staff and the nightmare of the anti-communist guerrillas.

The enormous MI-6 and MI-24 destined for the" development of Siberia" fooled no-one… these giants of the air were able to transport light tanks in the hold or by towing underneath. The Soviets experimented their airmobile doctrine successfully in Afghanistan, Ethiopia and Angola. The "Spetnatz, MI-24" duo caused great losses in the ranks of the Afghan guerrillas.

The quantity is allied with a certain quality and the West forces group based in Germany uses 300 Hind, 300 MI-8/17 and 50 MI-6 which can be supported by units from Rodina (in the mother country) in 24 hours. The end of

The MIL MI-17 makes up the framework of transport helicopters of the Russian armed forces. This type of helicopter was used intensively in Tchetchenie.

communism has brought the Red army into a period of decline and unprecedented budgetary difficulties; it is difficult to have a real idea of its true strength. The helicopters are continually working as they are used intensively in Tchetchenie and on the southern area of the CIS; and, according to some reports, they are still as efficient as ever. However the stock is aging, as is the majority of pilots, who are the same age as their machines and who have fought in Afghanistan. Only a massive injection of funds will allow the Russians to renew their stock with the Kamov-50 which represents an undeniable technological success. The base unit is the helicopter regiment or Otdielniy Vertoletniy Polk attached to a land army or a military region. For the MI-24 a regiment is generally made up of two squadrons (Eskadriliya) of approximately 20 Hind which work in groups of four to five machines. Currently, the organisation of the Russian helicopter forces is a rather grey area and consequently the battle order below is approximate. The treaty of Vienna concerning the reduction of conventional weapons allows Russia to use 890 armed helicopters and it seems that Russian aviation can put 989 in use.

Battle order:

Aerial Defence Troops V-PVO Voyska Protivovosdushnoy Oborony
235 and 436 independent transport squadrons on MI-8.
Air Force V-VS Voyenno-Vozdushnyye Sily.
Frontal aviation:
4th air arm at Rostov on the Don with 286 squadron (EW), 368 and 535 independent regiment.
15th air arm at Riga in Latvia with 249th regiment on MI-8.
16th air arm formerly in Germany with the 226th transport regiment on MI-8 and MI-6
76th air arm at St. Petersburg with
the 138th transport regiment on MI-8 and MI-6
and 227 squadron (EW) on MI-8.
Moscow military district.
269th transport regiment on MI-8 at Maloino.
285 squadron (EW) on MI-8 at Saransk.
297th combat regiment on MI-8 and MI-24 at Alabino.
378th transport regiment on MI-8 at Kiubinka.
Volga military district.
118th independent squadron on MI-8
and MI-6 at Dimitriyevka.
114th transport squadron at Samara.
Aviation school at Belashov on MI-2 and MI-8.
Independent units on MI-8 and MI-24.
172nd (Kasimovo), 225th (Protosovo), 258th (Luostari), 288th (Nivenskoye), 336th (Kaluga),
337th (ex East Germany exact area unknown).
It is not possible to have information concerning
the military districts of North Caucasus,
Oural, Siberia, Transbaikal and the far east,
these regions are not covered by the treaty of Vienna.

Stock: KAMOV-KA-50 "HOKUM" (on order),
270 MIL-MI-6 "HOOK", 1300 Mil MI-8/9/17 "HIP",
10 MIL-MI 10 "HARKE" (flying crane), 1450 MIL MI-24 HIND (in fact 989 theoretically in service conforming to the treaty of Vienna), MIL MI-28 "HAVOC" (on order),
35 MIL MI-26 HALO, 500 PZL MI-2.

An MIL MI-8 Hip, still with the USSR red star marking.

An MIL MI-6 Hook, an enormous transport helicopter and "beast of burden" of the Russian armed forces, is used in every area in the world under the colours of the UN among others.

Byelorussia

This country is very close to Russia as it has kept the red star on its craft. It has three combat regiments attached to the 5th Army of the guard, the 7th armoured and the 28th army and independent (EW) and liaison units. The stock consists of 26 MI-2, 35 MI-6, 140 MI-8, 78 MI-24, 14 MI-26.

Ukraine

The Ukraine has its own army aviation with roughly 400 craft in service. It is difficult to have an exact idea concerning the stock at present; numerous helicopters have been sold or scrapped because of a lack of fuel. Ukraine has 360 MI-8/17, 40 MI-6, 310 MI-24, 20 MI-26, 80 MI-2.
The old Soviet republics use a great many Russian helicopters. It is obviously difficult to have accurate information but whether in Armenia or in Tadzhikistan the MI-8/17 and MI-24 are used extensively. The Baltic countries use several MI-2 and MI-8.

SIKORSKY S-70 A/UH-60 BLACKHAWK

Because the Blackhawk, the principal medium of U S aerial attack, was the subject of a great deal of media attention as a result of documentaries and reports on the invasion of Grenada, fighting in Panama or humanitarian operations in Haiti, it has replaced the immortal Huey. Indeed the US army launched a programme for a machine able to transport the same number of soldiers but with improved performance and an anti crash element. The programme was delayed because of the Vietnam war, and it was in January 1972 that Sikorsky proposed his S-70 designated YUH-60, which flew for the first time on 17 October 1974. It was powered by two General Electric T-700 turbines driving a four-blade rotor, the YUH-60 had a very well streamlined cabin and the helicopter remarkable robustness. In December 1976, Sikorsky won the contract against its competitor the Boeing Vertol YUH-61. Production began in 1978 under the name UH-60 A Blackhawk and the first machines were delivered to the 101st Air Assault Division the following year. The introduction of the BlackHawk represented a real technological revolution and relegated the very competent Huey to the rank of "prehistoric". Officially conceived for 11 infantrymen the BlackHawk easily carried 20 and could transport heavy loads by cable in extreme conditions with a rather disconcerting ease. Equipped with a bulletproof tank, the UH-60 A was a machine with a surprising manoeuvrability. Throughout the years other modifications contributed to an increase in protection such as an exhaust to avoid AA missiles as well as chaff-launchers and an increasingly effective avionic. Some small wings can be mounted manually above the cabin door, this allows four extra tanks or weapon pylons to be carried. M-60 7.62mm machine guns or an M-134 minigun can be side mounted and there are several special versions in existence for MEDEVAC use. The tail rotor beam can fold up which means a BlackHawk can be put in the hold of a Lockheed C-5 Galaxy.

As new equipment was installed the UH-60 increased its weight and lost power, so Sikorsky, after abandoning the too expensive UH-60M programme, launched the UH-60L equipped with new T-700-GE-701C turbines each developing 1723hp. Powered in this way, the BlackHawk could even transport a Hummer vehicle by cable in its TOW version.

The first UH-60L flew in March 1988 and deliveries for the US Army are still being carried out to this day. The American land forces would have liked the use of 2262 BlackHawk, but as a result of budgetary restrictions they were only able to acquire 1400.

The UH-60Q, a new version, a real flying ambulance able to fly in all weathers, should replace models UH-60 A and L destined for medical evacuations. A single model was delivered to the Tennessee National Guard. Another original model is the VH-60N Presidential Hawk, nine examples of which are used by the Marine Corps to transport the President. Recognisable by its aerials the EH-60C is an electronic war machine 66 models of which have been delivered to helicopter brigades of the large US units. There are also versions derived from the BlackHawk in existence; the HH-60D NightHawk and MH-60G Pave Hawk destined for the USAAF SAR operations as well as the top secret MH-60K and AH-60 modified to operate with the 160th Special Operations Aviation Regiment which took part in the Gulf war.

A worthy successor to the Huey, the BlackHawk has also been widely ordered by various armed forces, generally under the name of S-70. Currently the craft is still being offered for export by Sikorsky. Australia, Korea and Japan build it under license.

Opposite: These BlackHawk of the 3rd Armoured division aviation brigade in Germany take off in formation.

The elegant silhouette of a BlackHawk of the 82nd Airborne stands out against the strange rocky formations in the Saudi desert.

Turkish commandos embarking a BlackHawk during operation STEEL led by the Turkish armed forces against the Kurds of the PKK.

Characteristics

For the UH-60 A BlackHawk

Rotor diameter: 16.36m
Turning rotor length: 19.76m
Length of fuselage: 15.26m
Engines: Two General Electric
T-700-GE-700 turbines each
developing 1560hp
Empty weight: 5118kg
Weight with full load: 9185kg
Internal fuel capacity: 1361 l
plus 1400 l fuselage extra tank
and two tanks under the pylons of 1703 l
Maximum speed: 296 km/h
Cruising speed: 268 km/h
Fuel efficient speed: 195km/h
Autonomy: 592 km,
with four tanks 2224 km
The BlackHawk can transport
20 infantrymen with its three-man crew.

This UH-60 A from 512 escuadrone of the Colombian army was delivered by the US army to fight against the drug cartels.

This BlackHawk from a medical company of the XVIII corps is being refuelled near Rafha in Saudi Arabia during the Gulf war.

ELECTRONIC WARFARE AND INFORMATION GATHERING

The term "electronic warfare" groups together two actions under the same name: operations with the aim of gaining information on the enemy and those designed to jam communications and enemy radar. If a war in central Europe should arise, the Red army has as its objective to neutralise a third of NATO HQ by destruction after location and another third by jamming communications within the first 24 hours. Some of these operations are carried out by means of helicopters: Mi-8 Ps, HIP-D, Mi-9 HIP-G, Mi-8 SMV HIP-J or Mi-8 PPA HIP-K carrying aerials along the fuselage beam.

The Americans use three helicopters per battalion, the EH-60c equipped with an ALQ-151 "Quick fix" jamming system.

France, with the Cougar HORIZON (a French acronym: Observation Helicopter Radar and Observation on Zone) is equipped with a large battle field observation programme. Jeopardised by the end of the cold war the programme was saved by the Gulf war where a PUMA ORCHIDEE (Airborne Investigation Radar Observation Post) the ancestor of the HORIZON, undertook 24 mis-

sions. A Puma guided a pack of AH-64 Apache at night on an Iraqi convoy. Without going into details, the Cougar HORIZON can be considered as a mini AWAC designed for battlefield surveillance.

Recognisable by its aerials on its fuselage beam, this electronic war EH-60 seen in the Gulf belong to the 82nd Airborne.

ISRAEL

Hardened by four bloody conflicts during which the State of Israel fought for its very survival, the Heyl Ha'Avir or Israeli Air force is considered as one of the best in the world. A mixture of realpolitik, daring, professionalism and advanced technology associated with the large financial aid from the US have made the Heyl Ha'Avir an organisation which has no rival in that part of the world. The helicopter units are in fact squadrons attached to the aviation. Every Israeli pilot has the certitude that everything will be done to save him in the event of any problem and that knowledge obviously has an effect on his performance. The story of a jet pilot, saved at the last minute and brought back from S. Lebanon to Israel by the landing gear of a Cobra goes some way to confirming that fact. Israeli helicopters are often engaged in operations against the Hezbollah in S.Lebanon..

An Apache AH-64 from the Tayeset 117 at Ramon.

An AH-1 Cobra from Tayeset 161 at Palmachim.

An Israeli mechanic checks the levels on a Hughes 500 D from Tayeset 190 at Ramat David.

Battle order:

Each air base has a section which has one or two helicopter squadrons (Tayeset) as well as fighter units.

1 squadron	- Tayeset 190 - : Hughes 500D (Ramat David)
8 squadron	- Tayeset 114 and 118 - : Yas'ur CH-53 (Tel-Nov)
15 squadron	- Tayeset 125 - : Bell 206 (Sde Dov)
25 squadron	- Tayeset 117 - : "Bourdon" : AH-64 (Ramon)
30 squadron	- Tayeset 124 - : AB-212 and UH-60
	Tayeset 127 - : AH-64 A
	Tayeset 160 - : "Green snake" AH-1
	Tayeset 161- : "Yellow snake" AH-1

(Palmachim. This base is Israel's principal helicopter base).
Advanced training squadron with Bell 212 at Hatzerim.

Stock: 50 Bell 212 Anafa (Heron), 35 Bell 206 Jet Ranger Saifan (Engoulevent), 40 Bell AH-1 Q/S/F/ Tsefa (Viper), 25 Hughes 500-MD TOW Lahatoot (Acrobat), 42 Mc Donnell Douglas AH-64 A Pethen (Cobra), 45 Sikorsky CH-53 A and D Yas'ur (Petrel), 10 Sikorsky UH-60 Nammer (Tiger).
As Israel is very discreet concerning its security, it is possible that the number of helicopters in service is greater than that given in this battle order.

THE ARAB WORLD

Morocco

Even though the conflict against the Polisario Front has lost a great deal of its intensity, there is still tension with Algeria. The helicopter units, attached to Al Quwwat al Jawwiya al Makiya Marakishiya or the Moroccan Royal Air force, they distinguished themselves during the war in the Sahara.

Stock: 2 AS-365 N Dauphin (VIP transport), 24 SA-342 K and SA-342 L Gazelle (reco and antitank), 30 SA-330 c and SA-330 G Puma (transport), 45 AB-205 A (transport), 17 AB-206 A/B (reconnaissance and liaison), 5 AB-212 (transport), 9 Elicotteri Meridonali CH-47C Chinook, 2 SA-315 Lama.

Tunisia

This N. African country has remained an oasis of tranquillity in a troubled region. It has an air force which regroups a squadron of transport and liaison helicopters the Al Quwwat al Jawwiya al Djoumhouria al Tunisia. Several Gazelle are equipped for ground attack.

Stock: 6 AS-350 B Ecureuil, 6 SA-342 k Gazelle, 12 AB-205 A, 6 UH-1H Iroquois, 5 Alouette II, 6 S-316 Alouette III.

Egypt

This country, which is one of the key countries n the Arab world, is very discreet concerning the state and the composition of its armed forces. It appears nonetheless that Egyptian pilots are very competent, contrary to their disastrous reputation during the sixties. Their stock consists of a great number of Russian helicopters, but the Egyptians build the Gazelle in Egypt and will receive some AH-64 Apache which will considerably increase the "muscle" of the Al Quwwat al Jawwiya al Misriya. Westland Commando are also used for electronic war.

Stock: 4 SA-342 K Gazelle (liaison), 75 SA-342 l (antitank), 2 Sikorsky S-61 (VIP), 15 CH-47 C Chinook, 18 Hiller UH-12E, 6 Mi-6 Hook (without doubt withdrawn from service), 40 Mi-8 HIP, 2 Sikorsky S-70 BlackHawk (VIP), 28 Westland Commando including 4 EW, 24 AH-64 Apache (12 on option).

Algéria

The Algerian air force or Al Quwwat al Jawwiya al Jaza'eriya is a very effective yet discreet air force. Few things show through the intense helicopter-led operations in the horrifying fight against the Islamic movements. Some Mi-24 and French fennec with night combat equipment would have been used. Apart from several French machines, the majority of the stock is of Russian origin.

Stock: 9 AS-550 Fennec, 5 SA-330 Puma, 4 Mil Mi-6 Hook, 12 Mil Mi-8 HIP (47 are on order), 24 Mi-24 Hind.
To face up to the Islamic guerrillas, some extra Mi-8 and Mi-24 are on order.

Libyan Chinook used in Chad.

Libya

Since the setbacks experienced against the Chad army supported by France, Libya seems to have lost its hegemonic impulses. Nonetheless, the number of aeroplanes and helicopters of the Al Quwwat al Jawwiya al Jammahiriyah al Arabia al Libya or Air force of the Arab Republic of Libya is impressive. However, because of a lack of qualified personnel and maintenance, a lot of the craft remain grounded. The Mi-24 belong to the air force, a fair number of transport helicopters and armed Gazelle are used by the land forces.

Stock: 2 Agusta A-109 (VIP), 2 AB-212, 1 Sikorsky S-61 (VIP), 7 Mi-8, 21 Mi-24 Hind, 35 SA-342 Gazelle, AB-47 G (certainly no longer in service), 5 AB-206 Jet Ranger, 12 CH-47C Chinook, 10 SA-316 Alouette III (certainly no longer in service).

Opposite: Egyptian Westland Commando.

Jordan

Considered to have one of the best air forces in the near-east the Al Quwwat al Jawwiya al Malakiya al Urduniya or Royal Jordanian Air Force has roughly 60 helicopters.

Battle order:

Operation Command:
Squadron 7: Cougar (Amman/Marka)
Squadron 8: S-70 and BO-105 CBS (Amman/Marka)
Squadron 10: AH-1 F (Amman/Marka)
Squadron 12: AH-1F (Amman/Marka)
Squadron 5 - Training Command-: Hughes 500D (Mafraq)

Stock: 11 AS-532 UL Cougar, 24 AH-1F Cobra, 2 Sikorsky S-70 A BlackHawk, 6 Hughes 500 D. 2 MBB BO-105 CBS. 18 UH-1H (in the course of being delivered).

Bahrain

The island state of Bahrain has 12 AB-212, 2 Bell 412 SP, 1 Sikorsky UH-60 A BlackHawk (VIP) and 8 AH-64 Apache are on order.

Syria

In a latent state of war with Israel and also having disputes with Turkey the Al Quwwat al Jawwiya al Arabia al'Souriya or Syrian Air Force is one of the units where secrecy is extremely highly respected. Apart from several Gazelle, it was towards Russia that Syria turned to construct its fleet of helicopters. The Gazelle performed very honourably during the war in Lebanon in 1982, destroying several Israeli tanks. The Syrians seized Mount Hermon in 1973 during a daring helicopter operation with the help of the Mi-8.

Stock: 55 Aerospatiale AS-342 L Gazelle, 10 Mi-6 Hook, approx. 100 Mi-8/17 Hip, 36 Mi-24 Hind, 20 PZL-Mi-2.

Iraq

Even though helicopters were extensively used during the conflict with Iran or during operations against Kurds or Shi-ites, it would appear that they were hardly used at all against the coalition forces during Desert Storm, apart from the initial attack on Kuwait city. Crushed by the UN embargo, the helicopters which survived the gulf war fly as part of counter-guerrilla operations. The Al Quwwat al Jawwiya al Iraqiya has roughly 300 machines.

Stock: 30 SA-342 L Gazelle, 10 SA-330 Puma, 3 AB-S-61 (VIP), 20 Bell 214 ST, 60 MBB-BO 105 C, 15 MBB/Kawasaki BK-117, 25 Mc Donnell Douglas MD-500d, 20 Mc Donnell Douglas MD-530 F, 10 Mi-6 Hook, 80 Mi-8 Hip, Service 20 Mi-24 Hind, 3 Mi-10 Harke (certainly withdrawn from service).

Kuwait

The Kuwaiti air force has been totally remodelled after its near destruction during the gulf war. It is now back to full capacity, enhanced by the combat experience that some Gazelle pilots gained.

Battle order:

Squadron 31 and 32 on SA-330 H Puma
Squadron 33 and 34 on SA-342 K/L Gazelle.
Squadron 62 on SA-332 B

Stock: 10 SA-342 K/L Gazelle, 7 SA-330 Puma, 4 AS-332 Super Puma.

Saudi Arabia

Because of its petrodollars, this country, which is the guardian of the Holy sites of Islam, has a not insignificant air force but it is one which suffers from a lack of maintenance personnel. It is often foreigners who maintain Saudi aircraft and helicopters and, in a war situation, this could have disastrous consequences on their operations. Just before the gulf war, Saudi Arabia built up its own army aviation, with approximately sixty ultramodern helicopters.

One of the ultra-modern S-70s in service in the Saudi armed forces.

Stock: 2 AS-365 Dauphin 2, 15 Bell 406 CS (Combat Scout), 12 AH-64 A Apache, 13 Sikorsky S-70 A-1 Desert Eagle, 8 S-70 A1I Desert Eagle (MEDEVAC) 8 Sikorsky UH-60A BlackHawk, 12 AB-205 A, 13 AB-206 A, 25 AB-212.

Qatar

This small, pro-Western emirate has 2 helicopter squadrons, based at Doha, with 6 squadron on Gazelle and 9 squadron on Westland Commando and Super Puma. 8 squadron on Commando is destined for maritime anti surface fighting but can use its helicopters for assault missions. The Qatari were involved in the gulf war and notably in the Iraqi attack on Al Kafji in December 1990.

A beautiful formation of Qatari Gazelle. Note the very particular desert camouflage.

Stock: 2 SA-341 K Gazelle, 14 SA-342 L Gazelle, 6 AS-332 F Super Puma, 4 Westland Commando MK-2.

Lebanon

The Al Quwwat al Jawwiya al Lubnaniya which did not survive the long Lebanese civil war is in the process of being re-formed with essentially French and American material.

Stock: 3 SA-342 Gazelle, 9 SA-330 Puma, 7 AB-212, 2 SE-313 Alouette II, 6 SA 316 B Alouette III. 16 UH-1 Iroquois (plus 16 on order from the stock of the US Army).

United Arab Emirates

Regrouping the air forces of Abu Dhabi, Dubai and Sharjah, the emirates have established their HQ at Abu Dhabi. The most recent acquisition to their stock is the formidable Apache which from now on will be put into operation next to older French models. The rise of power of Iran and several Saudi territorial claims must worry the oil rich emirates. The confederation organised its means of defence into two great commands: west and central, each one regroups helicopter units.

Stock: Abu Dhabi: 1 AS-350 Ecureuil, 11 SA-342 J Gazelle, 11 SA-330 F Puma, 9 AS-332 Super Puma, 1 AB-206 B Jet Ranger, 20 AH-64 Apache (plus ten recently ordered). Dubai: 1 AS-365 N-1 Dauphin, 6 AB-205 A, 6 AB-206A/B/L Jet Ranger, 4 Bell 212, 4 Bell 214, 6 MBB BO-105 S. Sharjah: 3 Bell 206.

The Yemen

Reunified in May 1990, the Yemen is attempting to reform an air force worthy of the name after a bloody civil war. Most of its machines are of Russian or Italian origin.

Stock: 2 AB-204B, 6 AB-206B Jet Ranger, 6 AB-212, 50 Mi-8 Hip, 15 Mi-24 Hind.

Oman

Under the energetic spirit of Sultan Qabus, educated in Great Britain, the Sultanate of Oman, guardian of the straits opposite Iran has reliable, well-trained armed forces which are often supervised by British personnel.

Battle order:

Squadron 3: Bell 205, 212 and 214 (Salalah)
Squadron 14: Bell 205 and 206 (Salalah)
Royal Flight: Super Puma (Muscate).

Stock: 2 AS-332 Super Puma, 20 AB-205A, 3 AB-206 A, 2 AB-212, 10 AB-214 S/T.

HEAVY HELICOPTERS

At the beginning of the sixties, technological progress meant that more powerful engines were being mounted in more impressive airframes. This was how a new generation of helicopters with very precise functions came into existence. Heavy helicopters (1) are real monsters capable of transporting more than forty soldiers, artillery pieces and ammunition or of transporting more than 5 tonnes. They completely modified airmobile combat as was proved in the seventies when Russian Mi-6s transported light AS-85 tanks behind Somali lines. This daring manoeuvre changed the course of the Ogaden war.

During the Falklands, a Chinook, the only survivor of the Atlantic Conveyor sunk by the Argentineans, was used far beyond its potential by transporting 85 soldiers. "Heavy" helicopters, generally receiving less media attention than attack helicopters, are sorts of flying cranes or combat vehicles. They have a position of extreme importance in the strategy of the chiefs of staff. Indeed several machines can refuel an armoured division very quickly or, in several rotations, drop a complete battalion on the enemy's flank or rear. These machines can also be used in the event of a natural disaster for bringing supplies and aid into isolated zones. Everyone remembers the courage of the Russian MI-26 pilots who sacrificed their lives to drop liquid concrete onto the reactor at Chernobyl. Few heavy helicopters have been developed but old airframes are constantly being updated and benefit from the latest technical developments.

(1) In fact in NATO the CH-53 and the Chinook are considered as medium helicopters but their load capacity is near 8 tonnes.

First of the heavy Russian helicopters the MI-6 "HOOK" was exported to a number of countries.

An RAF Chinook takes off from Vaêrlose in Denmark opposite a line of German CH-53. Both types of NATO "heavy" helicopters are represented on this photo.

SIKORSKY S-65/CH-53

Conceived at the request of the US Marine Corps the prototype of the S-65 flew for the first time on 14th October 1964 and began service the following year. The craft is marked out by a large, box-shaped cabin, accessible by a rear ramp allowing access for light vehicles.

Widely used by the Marine corps, the CH-53 in its A and D versions saw action in Vietnam, Grenada, Panama and Lebanon. These days the CH-53 is the most impressive helicopter used in the west. The Bundeswehr has 110 of these machines in service. The history of the German CH-53 starts in 1968 when the Sikorsky won the competition which planned to replace the H-34 and Piasecki H-21 in the Heeresflieger.

Apart from the first two machines delivered by Sikorsky, 20 models named CH-53G were built by the VFW-Fokker consortium, followed by 90 others manufactured in Germany. The first flight of a CH-53G took place at Speyer in 1971 and the craft entered service in March 1973 within the Heeresflieger regiment 35 at Mendig. Two other regiments, the Heeresfliegerregiment 15 and 35 were formed with CH-53G which thus became the principal multi-function helicopter of the Bundeswehr. In the Fallschirmjäger rapid intervention units placed at the disposition of NATO or WEU, the CH-53G/Wiesel light armoured antitank duo is from now on inseparable. A complete modernisation programme of the airframes is envisaged. The CH-53G will remain in the Bundeswehr long after the year 2000.

Austria acquired two S-65C in the sixties, but their utilisation cost shortened their career and both craft were sold to Israel. Israel acquired 33 SC-65C in 1969 and 10 CH-53 A in 1991 coming from USMC surplus. Able to be refuelled during flight, the Israeli CH-53 took part in a number of war operations.

One of the most spectacular took place during the 1973 war when commando jeeps dropped behind Syrian lines by CH-53s and Super Frelons destroyed Iraqi T-55 and T-62s sent to reinforce the Golan Heights. A vast modernisation programme named CH-53 2000 or Yas'ur 2000 (Albatross) will permit the Israeli CH-53 to remain operational until the next cen-

Exercise "COLD GROUSE 95": first deployment of the new NATO airmobile division, this was a great gathering of CH-53 of the Bundeswehr, this craft is the principal one of German airmobile deployment.

tury. Carried out by the IAI Mata Helicopter division, the programme comprises the installation of the EW Elira system, a digitalised multi functional cockpit, an automatic pilot and a mission computer. The first CH-53 2000 began service in 1993.

Characteristics

Rotor diameter: 22m
Turning rotor length: 26.90m
Length of fuselage: 20.47m
Engines: Two General Electric T-64 GE-16 turbines developing 3435hp
Normal weight at take off: 15976kg
Fuel capacity: 2384 l
Internal load capacity: 3629kg
With cable: 5897kg
Maximum speed: 314km/h
Cruising speed: 277 km/h
Mission radius: 413 km for an autonomy of 4 hours.
The CH-53 is capable of carrying 50 equipped soldiers, meaning that three craft in one rotation can place a company on the terrain.

BOEING VERTOL HELI

The Chinook, distant descendant of the "bananas" of the Algerian war, is recognisable by its particular silhouette. It is a reliable craft, beginning its legendary history in Vietnam and since has been constantly updated technologically and used by a number of countries. Developed by Vertol, the two rotor concept, assessed on the Piaseckis had given satisfaction in Korea and Algeria and the firm built a new prototype, the V-144, or YHC-1 in its military designation, which flew the first time on 21st September 1961. The following year, under the name CH-47A Chinook the machine began its brilliant career in the US Army. By placing the engines outside and by mounting the two large rotors above the fuselage, the Vertol engineers left enough space in the cabin to transport 55 equipped soldiers or one or two light vehicles. The crew consisted of two pilots and a loadmaster.

The Chinook is also an assault helicopter, and is used for supporting "drops" in enemy zones. It can be armed with a minigun or machine guns fired through the rear ramp or side doors. The first Chinooks had just one transport hook but the latest versions have three, thus allowing an artillery piece or a light tank to be transported in a "sling". A synchronisation system also prevents the two large rotors from touching each other. The first generation, that is to say 354 CH-47A went to Vietnam as part of the US Army and gave total satisfaction. 108 more powerful CH-47Bs with increased rotor size, followed.

This did not stop Boeing from developing a new model, the CH-47C equipped with new engines, extra tanks (which in fact the previous models had) and an increased capacity to withstand crashes. With 182 examples of versions A and B re-modernised and 88 new machines, the US Army thus acquired 270 CH-47C.

This model flew for the first time on 14th October 1967 and the US govt. gave the go-ahead for export. The craft had an immediate success and the Chinook is without doubt, the most widely used medium helicopter in the world. (see page 124). The RAF adopted it under the name Chinook HC-MK1 and improved it with a cockpit adapted with NVG (Night Vision Goggles), an automatic

The Chinook HC-2 is the latest version of this type of craft in use in the RAF, which will use 49 machines.
A new dark olive green camouflage has been adapted on the HC-2. Here, three machines take off during operation COLD GROUSE 95 in Denmark.

COPTER CH-47 CHINOOK

Characteristics

CH-47D

Rotor diameter: 18.29m
Turning rotor length: 30.14m
Length of fuselage: 15.54m
Engines:
Two Textron Lycoming
T-55-L-712 turbines
each developing 4378hp
Empty weight: 10151kg
Weight with maximum load:
22679kg
Maximum speed: 298km/h
Cruising speed: 256km/h.

An Italian CH-47 from the grupo Antares is about to land on Spanish soil during exercise TRAMONTANA 94.

fuel fire fighting system and glass fibre blades. The Italian company Elicoterri Meridonali obtained the manufacturing license for the Italian army and supplies clients in the near east and the Mediterranean.

The improvements made for export purposes led the US Army to order 472 CH-47D which is the last version brought up to standard D or new machine standard. The first of these began service in the 101st Air Assault in May 1982. In operations, the CH-47D and its RAF version designated HC-MK 2 can carry up to 10341 kg underneath or transport 6308 kg in the cabin. This capacity for transporting ammunition and heavy loads and in all weathers was particularly useful during the gulf war where US and British Chinooks accomplished Special Forces infiltration missions (SAS) and resupplied batteries with multiple rocket launchers.

A version destined for the Special Forces, the MH-47E SOA, able to be refuelled in flight and loaded with electronics and counter-measure equipment, is in service with the 160th Special Operations Aviation group at Fort Campbell and the 1/245th battalion SOA of the National Guard at Oklahoma. Despite its age, the airframe of the Chinook has stayed very effective and will doubtless be able to accommodate new modifications which will mean that this machine will fly well beyond the year 2000.

These two CH-47 C from FAMET sir up the dust of Andalucia during exercise GALIA 88 near Cordoue.

123

User countries

Argentina: 3 CH-47 C one of which was captured by the British in the Falklands.
Australia: 4 CH-47 D
Canada: 9 withdrawn from service and sold to the Netherlands.
South Korea: 24 CH-47 D
Spain: 9 CH-47 C and 9 CH-47 D.
Egypt: 15 CH-47c (Elicoterri meridionali).
Greece: 9 CH-47 C from the Elicoterri meridionali in the process of being transformed into CH-47C at Boeing.
Iran: 68 CH-47C delivered by Elicoterri meridionali. Used intensively during the Iran-Iraq war it is difficult to know the remainder of craft in service.
Italy: 38 CH-47C 26 of which are modernised.
Japan: 42 CH-47 J (CH-47D manufactured under license by Kawasaki).
Libya: 34 CH-47C (Elicoterri meridionali).
Morocco: 12 CH-47C (Elicoterri).
Nigeria: 5 ordered but not delivered because of non-payment.
The Netherlands: 13
United Kingdom: 35 HCMK-1 being transformed to HC-MK-2 and 14 HC-MK-2.
Singapore: 6 CH-47 D on order.
Taiwan: 3 civilian Boeing 234 MLR but used by the army.
Thailand: 3 CH-47 A and 12 CH-47 D on order.
USA: 472 CH-47 D and 32 MH-47 D SOA.

On opposite page: A Chinook from the aviation brigade of the XVIII Corps (Airborne) lands for refuelling during the gulf war after bringing back some Iraqi prisoners.

101st Air assault in the gulf.

The "beast of burden" of many of the world's air forces.

A Spanish craft during exercise TRAMONTAN.

A Japanese craft from the 1st Herikoputataï.

Greeks at the Megara base.

British, in the service of the UN at Ploce in Croatia.

Italian from the famous Antares group seen with an ALAT Gazelle during FARFADET 92.

Australian, before their withdrawal from service.

The end of the cold war drove a great number of countries to greatly reduce their defence budgets, this led to the dissolution of a third of the large mechanised formations which made up the armoury of the Atlantic Alliance. In addition, the threat represented by the Red Army changed into one of "low intensity" on peripheral NATO territories which necessitated the creation of forces much more flexible than armoured divisions. From 1992, four main countries of NATO decided to create an airmobile division which would be the forerunner of the NATO rapid reaction force. This division is made up of the Belgian para-commando brigade, the 31st Luftlande (German brigade), the 11th Lucthmobiele (Dutch brigade and the 24th airmobile (British brigade). The division was operational in Autumn 1995 and exercise Cold Grouse in Denmark will be its first major operational mission. A stock of 193 helicopters work for the division and the following table gives the exact strength for 1996 and that programmed for the year 2000. The number of helicopters will therefore be 232.

Some CH-53 G from the new German helicopter heavy transport brigade, heavy mortar section and vehicles of the Dutch 11th Luchtmobiele brigade.

A Puma from 230 squadron of the RAF with a new camouflage waits for Belgian para-commandos to embark.

BILE DIVISION

	1996	2000
Transport TUE, CH-53, Cougar, Puma	70	89
Antitank A-109, BO-105, Lynx	38	32
Attack AH-64 Apache	12	38
Observation A-109, Gazelle, Lynx BO-105	73	73
	193	232

*Liaison is undertaken
by these Dutch Alouette III
or German or Dutch BO-105.*

*Until the introduction of Apaches in 1997,
the division antitank reserve unit is ensured
by Belgian Agusta 109 Tow of the 18th battalion.*

MIL MI-6 "HOOK"

The development of the MIL Mi-6 started in 1954 when the Red Army and Aeroflot wanted to acquire a vast transport helicopter. When it made its first flight in 1957 the Mi-6 was then the largest helicopter in the world. The first Russian helicopter powered by turbines the Mi-6 T, named "Hook" by NATO, won several records and was the first helicopter to exceed 300km/H. The large detachable blades increased the performance of the rotor by 20% and decreased fuel consumption at the same time as increasing speed.

Five prototypes were built and 30 craft began service in the Red Army. The Hook is capable of carrying 75 equipped infantrymen or 41 stretchers in its MEDEVAC version. The rear doors open hydraulically and a winch with a tensile strength of 800kg can help with loading. The floor of the hold can bear a weight of 2000kg per square metre, which means light tanks can be transported. The crew is made up of 5 men: two pilots, a mechanic, navigator and a radio operator. Some craft are armed with 12;7mm machine guns in the nose whereas other versions have a weather radar. 800 Mi-6 were built and, as it was a symbol of Russian power in the seventies, it was widely exported. It even changed the course of the Ogaden war by transporting light tanks behind Somali lines. Capable of some outstanding feats, the Mi-6 was modified by the Red Army into a flying command post for all air operations. Two versions are in existence, the Mil Mi-6VKP or "Hook-B" and the Mil Mi-22 or "Hook-C".

Apart from extra aerials and the installation of a great number of electronics, the silhouette of the craft has not changed. These last two versions have not been exported.

Despite its massive 42 tonnes, this Mi-6 is nonetheless elegant in flight.

Characteristics

Rotor diameter: 35m. Wings: 15.30m
Turning rotor length: 41.74m
Length of fuselage: 33.18m
Engines: Two PNPP "Aviadvigatel"
Soloviev D-25V turbines each developing 5500hp.
Empty weight: 27240 kg - Weight with full load: 42500 kg
Internal fuel capacity: 6315 l plus 3490 l in cabin reservoir plus 12000 l in external reservoirs.
12 tonnes can be transported in cabin and 9 tonnes towed underneath.
Maximum speed: 300 km/h - Cruising speed: 250 km/h
Autonomy: 1450 km.

This impressively powerful MI-6 "Hook" takes off from a terrain south of Moscow. In spite of the existence of the yet more effective MI-26, the Hook is still very much appreciated by its crews.

MIL MI-26 "HALO"

Conceived to replace the Mi-6, the Mi-26 Halo, despite its slightly smaller size, is more powerful than its predecessor. The size of the hold is near that of a C-130, which means that the Mi-26 is the largest helicopter in service in the world. The first prototype flew on 14th December 1977 and the craft was received by the Red Army in 1985 within an evaluation squadron. Delivery to units began in 1985.

Using advanced techniques in the gear boxes and special aluminium-Lithium alloys the Mi-26 weighs 1000kg less than the Mi-6 but its two D-136 turbines give it twice the power.

The Halo can therefore transport twice the load of the Mi-6. In addition to its five-man crew, the Mi-26 can carry 80 infantrymen or 60 stretchers. Some PC flying versions, as for the Mi-6, will without doubt be put into service, but they have not yet been identified. It seems that a version for refuelling in flight, the Mi-26TZ, has been ordered.

The Mi-26 has been used in Tchetchenie by the Russian army and Russian and Ukrainian machines with UN colours have also been seen in Somalia, Cambodia and Yugoslavia.

India is the only foreign operator of the MI-26 as is proved here, this MI-26 of 126 squadron of the IAF flies above Chandigha.

Characteristics

Rotor diameter: 32m - Turning rotor length: 40m
Length of fuselage: 33.73m
Engines: Two ZMDB "Progress"
Lotarev D-136 turbines developing 11240hp
Empty weight: 28200 kg - Weight with full load: 56000kg
Internal fuel capacity: 12000
Maximum load: 20 tonnes
Maximum speed: 295km/h - Cruising speed: 255 km/h
Maximum autonomy: 2000km

Russian or Ukrainian MI-26s are used to UN missions where their great transporting capacities work wonders. Here, a Russian MI-26 with the white colours of the UN is seen at Mogadishu airport.

CENTRAL ASIA

An area between the Muslim world and the Fare East, this vast region, apart from the latent conflict between India and Pakistan, is familiar with a number of civil wars.

Bangladesh

The Bangladesh Defence Force Air Wing or Bangladesh Biman Bahini has three helicopter squadron, squadron 1 on Mi-8/17 squadron 18 on Bell 206 L and squadron 31 (VIP) on Bell 212 and Mi-8.

Stock: 2 bell 206 L, 10 Bell 212, 7 Mi-8, 4 Mi-17, 3 UH-1H.

A beautiful view of an MI-8 from 1 squadron of the Bangladesh Air Force. These helicopters often work in aid of people affected by cyclones which regularly strike the Bay of Bengal.

Afghanistan

Developed by the Soviets, the formidable combat force of eight helicopter squadrons crumbled after their withdrawal because of lack of spare parts and maintenance. The remainder of craft are nonetheless used intensively by the various factions which are fighting against each other for power.

Stock: These figures are approximate.
12 Mi-4 Hound (probably withdrawn from service).
45 Mi-8/17 Hip, 25 Mi-24 Hind.

Sri Lanka

The few helicopters of this small air force are engaged permanently n the ferocious civil war between the National Army and the Tamoul rebels. Heavily armed helicopters patrol above the Jafna peninsula where they attempt to intercept small boats bringing ammunition and reinforcements to the rebels.

Battle order:

Squadron N°4: Bell 206/212/412 SP (Colombo)
Squadron N°6: Mi-17 (Vavuniya).

Stock: 2 AS-365 C Dauphin 2, 6 Bell 206 A, Jet Ranger, 12 Bell 212, 4 Bell 412, 3 Mi-17 Hip.

Two helicopters of the Sri Lanka air force during operations against the Tamoul rebels. Both are equipped with 12.7mm FN Herstal HMP machine gun pods. The small Bell 206 also has a rocket magazine whereas the AB-212 has a door gunner.

Iran

Little is known concerning the strength of the air force f this Islamic republic, which in the last few years has been turning towards Russia for the purchase of its material.

Despite very severe losses during the Iran/Iraq war, the army aviation of Iran uses a high number of helicopters including the Bell model 214 Isfahan specially developed for the army of the Shah. It is possible that some Mi-24s delivered by the Russians or seized during the Gulf war from the Iraqis are in service.

Stock: 20 AB-205, 80 AB-206A/B, 30 Bell 212, 180 Bell 214 A/C, 100 AH-1J.

India

A giant country, India is also a military giant and the Bharatiya Vayu Sena or Indian Air Force is considered the best in Asia. It is divided into five large geographical commands and also the Maintenance Command which regroups a large number of helicopters. There is a light army aviation which only uses light machines such as the Cheetah (Lama) or the Chetak (Alouette III) made under license.

MI-26 of squadron 26 at take off.

Battle order: *Bharatiya Vayu Sena*

Squadron 104: Mi-35 Hind (Pathankot)
Squadron 109: Mi-8 (Delhi)
Squadron 3: Mi-8/17 (Chandigarh)
Squadron 26: Mi-26 Halo (Chandigarh)
The bases of the following units have not been localised.
Squadrons 36, 105, 107, 110, 111, 118, 119, 120, 121, 128, 129, 130, 151, 152: Mi-8 Hip
Squadrons 112, 114, 115: Chetak
Squadron 116, 125: Mi-25/35 Hind
The flying school at Bangalore uses all types of helicopters of the IAF.
Indian Army Air Corps
Squadrons 659, 660, 661 and 662: Hal Cheetah
Squadrons 104, 107, 111, 112, 113, 114, 115, 116, 117: Hal Chetak.

Stock: 2 AS-365 Dauphin. 10 Hal Cheetah in the air force and 50 in the air corps. 50 Hal Chetak in the air force and 100 in the air corps. 60 Mi-8 Hip. 37 Mi-17 HIP. 12 Mi-25 Hind. 20 Mi-35 Hind. 10 Mi-26 Halo.

A patrol of "HIND" MI-35 from 104 squadron.

A Cobra of squadron 32 in flight.
Pakistani pilots have and excellent reputation and often serve "on loan" for other Muslim countries.

Pakistan

To stand up to its old enemy, India, Pakistan has impressive armed forces and has an independent land forces light aviation, the HQ is at Dhamial. The principal attack helicopter is the Cobra whereas various Russian, French and American craft serve in transport and assault squadrons.

Battle order:

Squadron 2: UH-1H (Lahore)
Squadron 4: Mi-8 (Dhamial)
Squadron 6: UH-1H and AB-205 (Dhamial)
Squadron 8: Alouette III and Lama (Dhamial)
Squadron 9: Alouette III (Peshawar)
Squadron 21: Puma and UH-1H (Multan)
Squadron 24: Puma (Multan)
Squadron 25: Puma (Dhamial)
Squadron 31: AH-1F (Multan)
Squadron 32: AH-1F (Multan)

An MI-8 from squadron 4 waits with all its doors open for the mechanic to give it a maintenance check.

Stock: 25 SA-330 F/L Puma, 12 AB-205/UH-1H, 12 Bell 47G, 10 Bell 206B, 20 AH-1F Cobra, 8 Mi-8 Hip, 24 SA-316 B and Iar-316B Alouette III, 18 SA-315 Lama.

133

THE FAR EAST

The Japanese self defence force uses its own domestic army aviation the Rikujyo Jietai. The majority of these models are American but built under license in the land of the rising sun by Fuji or Kawasaki.

Battle order:

North Army. Hokubu Homentaï (Sapporo, Hokkaïdo)
North command squadron.
Hokubu Homen Hikotaï: OH-6
Helicopter squadron of north command.
Hokubu homen Herikoputataï: UH-1H
7th squadron. 7th Hikotaï: OH-6 and UH -1H
11th squadron. 11th Hikotaï: OH-6 and UH-1H
1st antitank squadron.
1st Taisensha Herikoputataï: AH-1 S and OH-6D
2nd squadron. 2nd Hikotaï: 0H-6 and UH-1H
5th squadron. 5th Hikotaï: OH-6 and UH-1H

North-east Army. Tohuku Homentaï (Sendaï, Honshu)
North east command squadron
(Tohuku Homen Hikotaï) OH-6.
Helicopter squadron of north east command.
Tohuku Homen Herikoputataï: UH-1H
2nd antitank squadron.
2nd Taisensha Herikoputataï: AH-1S and OH-6D
6th squadron. 6th Hikotaï: OH-6
9th squadron 9th Hikoaï: OH-6

The Cobra is the principal attack helicopter.

Each army has two squadron of OH-6 used for observation and liaison.

A naval machine but used by the Rikujyo Jieitai, the Vertol Kawasaki 107/II is used for troop transport.

East Army. Tobu Homentaï (Ichigaya, Honshu)
East command squadron.
Tobu Homen Hikotaï: OH-6
Helicopter squadron of east command.
Tobu Homen Herikoputataï: UH-1H
1st squadron. 1st Hikotaï: OH-6
4th antitank squadron. 4th Taisensha Herikoputataï:
AH-1S and OH-6D
12th squadron. 12th Hikotaï : OH-6

Central Army. Chubu Homentaï (Itami, Honshu)
Squadron of central command.
Chubu Homen Hikotaï: OH-6
Helicopter squadron of cêntral command.
Chubu Homen Herikoputataï: UH-1H
3rd squadron. 3rd Hikotaï: OH-6
10th squadron. 10th Hikotaï: OH-6
13th squadron. 13th Hikotaï: OH-6

West Army. Seïbu Homentaï (Kengun, Kyushu)
West command squadron.
Seibu Homen Hikotaï: OH-6
Helicopter squadron of West command.
Seibu homen Herikoputataï: UH-1H and KV-1O7/11
8th squadron. 8th Hikotaï: OH-6
4th squadron 4th Hikotaï: OH-6
101st mixed squadron.
101st Hikotaï: UH-1H and KV-107/II (Okinawa)
1st helicopter brigade.
Daï-Ichi Herikoputataï (Kisarasu, Honshu)
Special unit: AS-332 L (Tokubetu Yuso Hikotaï)
1st helicopter group.
1st Herikoputataï: CH-47 J, OH-6, KV-107/II
2nd helicopter group. 2nd Herikoputataï: OH-6, KV-107/II
The Akeno school of aviation at Honshu regroups all types of craft.

Stock: 3 AS-332L Super Puma, 25 UH-1B, 144 UH-1H, 85 AH-1J cobra, 36 CH-47J Chinook, 54 KV-107/II, 33 Hughes Th-55 J, 218 OH-6D, 65 OH-6J.

*An impressive take off for these CH-47
of the 1st helicopter brigade.*

North Korea

The air force of North Korea is without doubt the most mysterious in the world. The majority of the helicopters are Russian but North Korea was widely talked about several years ago because of its acquisition, through a German arms dealer, a large quantity of Hughes 300 and McDonnell Douglas MD-500 D destined for special operations.

Stock: 10 Hughes 300, 70 Mc Donnell Douglas MD-500D, 20 Mi-8 Hip, 20 Mi-24 Hind.

South Korea

To face up to its dangerous neighbour to the north, South Korea maintains a sizable army, one branch of this is light aviation of the army. The majority of the material is American.

Stock: 3 AS-332L Super Puma, 68 AH-1F/J Cobra, 20 UH-1H, 18 CH-47D Chinook, 140 Mc Donnell Douglas MD-500D, 45 Mc Donnell Douglas MD-500 M/D/Tow, AH-64 Apache (negotiations in progress for 37 craft) UH-60 P BlackHawk (22 delivered which will be followed by 80 constructed in S. Korea).

China

It is difficult to have accurate information concerning China, which in theory has the fourth largest air force in the world. Despite attempts at modernisation, the majority of the stock of the *Zhongkuo Shenmin Taifang Tsunputai* or Air force of the popular army is obsolete. China has constructed several models under license including the Super Frelon and Dauphin.

Stock: 8 S-342 L Gazelle, 6 AS-332 L Super Puma, 25 SA-365-Dauphin (Harbin Z-9), 30 Mi-8 Hip, 25 Mi-17 Hip, 20 Sikorsky S-70 C-II BlackHawk.

Taiwan

China has not yet renounced its intention to conquer Taiwan, which it considers to be an integral part of its territory. Tension has been mounting over the last few years because of mutual claims on the archipelagos in the China sea. Taiwan remains a stronghold. There is an army aviation in the process of being restructured with ultra-modern American equipment.

Stock: 55 Bell UH-1H Iroquois, 10 Bell 47G, 30 Bell OH-58D Kiowa warrior, 50 Bell AH-1W Super Cobra, 3 CH-47D Chinook.

*Taiwan is the only country, apart from USA,
to use the highly sophisticated Kiowa Warrior.*

SOUTH EAST ASIA

Burma

To face up to its many ethnic guerrilla groups, Burma turned toward China which gave it considerable technical assistance. The majority of its helicopters however come from the west.

Stock: 12 Bell UH-1H, 6 PZL-Mi-2, 32 PZL-W3 Sokol, 10 SA-216 B Alouette III.

Thailand

A sizable stock of more than 300 helicopters which is divided between the Royal Thai Air Force, the army and the border police, the border being heavy militarised.

Battle order: *Royal Thai Air Force.*

2nd squadron (Lopburi):
201st squadron: S-58T
203 squadron: UH-1H
Royal Flight: Bell 212/412
25 UH-1H, 1 Bell 212, 1 Bell 412 and 17 Sikorsky S-58T
Royal Thai Army: 70 Bell UH-1 B/D/H, 10 Bell 206A/B, 24 Bell 212, 4 Bell 412, 8 AH-1F Cobra, 12 CH-47D Chinook
Royal Thai Border Police: 18 Bell UH-1H, 14 Bell 206, 13 Bell 212.

Cambodia

Following an agreement which has theoretically put an end to the civil war, several Mi-8 and 17 of the Kampuchea Liberation Army have been put under the control of the UN and 4 Mi-24 Hind have been forbidden from flying.

Indonesia

In spite of its oil reserves, this immense country has a relatively limited air force, the Tentara Nasional Indonesia-Angkata Udara has several squadrons of American and French machines. The army has its own light aviation, the Tentara Nasional Indonesia-Angkatan Darat. Puma, BO-105 and Bell 412 are assembled locally by the firm IPTN.

Battle order: Air Force

Squadron 6: Puma and Super Puma
Squadron 17: Puma and S-58 T
The organigram of Indonesian ALAT is not known but there are roughly sixty helicopters.

Stock: 10 IPTN-NAS-330J Puma, 7 IPTN-NAS-332B Super Puma, 10 Sikorsky S-58, 12 Bell 205 A, 26 IPTN Bell 412, 13 IPTN MBB BO-105, 16 UH-60 BlackHawk on order.

Brunei

This small Sultanate has three squadrons. The first is equipped with 11 Bell 212/214 and the second with 5 BO-105 CB. The third squadron uses 2 Bell 206 Jet Ranger and SF-260 aeroplanes.

Singapore

The island state of Singapore, an important commercial power in S.E. Asia, has the means of having a sizable air force and is equipped with approximately thirty helicopters.

Battle order:

Squadron 120 "Condor": UH-1H
Squadron 123 "Sunbird": Fennec
Squadron 124: Ecureuil
Squadron 125: "Starling": Super Puma

Stock: 6 AS-350 B Ecureuil,
9 AS-550 C-2 Fennec (antitank),
10 AS-550 U2 Fennec (gun), 16 AS-332 Super Puma,
16 Bell UH-1H, 20 Bell 406 CS (Combat Scout)
6 Boeing model 234 Chinook.

Malaysia

This Muslim country has several squadron (3,7 and 10) where Alouette III and Sikorsky S-61 naval helicopters are mixed. The latter is known locally as "Nuri" and is adapted to transport and assault missions.

Stock: 5 Bell 47G, 33 Sikorsky S-61 Nuri,
24 SA-316 Alouette III.

The Philippines

Confronted with communist and Islamic armed opposition, the Philippines maintains a sizable helicopter force whose pilots are particularly well-trained in anti-guerilla operations. The craft are dependent on the Philippine AF or Hokbong Himpapawid ng Pilipinas.

Battle order:

20th Air Commando Squadron: S-76 and AUH-76
18th Tactical Air Support Squadron: MD-500 MG
205th Helicopter Wing with the 210th and
211th helicopter squadrons: AB-205, UH-1H, Bell 214.
252nd Helicopter squadron : Bell 205, BO-105, S-70,
S-76 and Puma.

Stock: 1 SA-330 Puma (VIP), 30 Bell 205 and UH-1H,
1 Bell 212, 1 Bell 214, 10 MBB-BO-105, 1 Sikorsky S-70,
2 Sikorsky S-76, 8 Sikorsky AUH-76.

Laos

A small country hemmed in between two powerful neighbours, Laos has one Mi-6 Hook and nine Mi-8 Hip.

Vietnam

The end of the Soviet Union led to a slight loss of power of the Khon Quan Nhan Dan Vietnam. Helicopters of essentially Russian origin are attached to the 916th helicopter regiment at Hoa Lac.

Stock: 10 Mi-6 Hook, 55 Mi-8 Hip, 30 Mi-24 Hind.

AFRICA

This continent witnessed the first great helicopter operations in Algeria in the fifties, and also the Portuguese and Rhodesian colonial wars where the helicopter played an important role. The stock of helicopters is in the image of Africa itself, in other words in rather a sorry state. Corruption, lack of funds and spare parts have grounded most craft except several presidential helicopters, often piloted by mercenaries. Apart from Nigeria and Angola, which with money from oil or Russian aid, have several units, most countries have very few reliable machines. The Mi-8 and 17 are particularly well-adapted to Africa because of their hardiness yet ease of maintenance. Rwandan pilots knew how to keep their Gazelle and Alouette at an operational level during fighting in the civil war. Often in Africa "pieces of string" can work miracles and craft fly in conditions that would make a Western engineer's hair curl.

But sometimes it works!

Two MI-8 from Djibouti.
These craft were operational against the Afar rebellion.

Stock: ANGOLA: 11 SA-342 L Gazelle, 13 AS-565 Panther, 30 IAR-316 Alouette III, 30 Mi-8/17 Hip, 20 Mi-25/35 Hind, 2 SA-315 Lama. BENIN: 2 AS-350 Ecureuil. BOTSWANA: 2 AS-350 Ecureuil, 5 Bell 412. BURKINA FASO: 2 AS-350 Ecureuil, 1 Mi-8, 2 Mi-17. BURUNDI: 2 AS-342L Gazelle, 4 SA-316B Alouette. CAMEROON: 1 AS-365 N Dauphin 2, 4 SA-342 L Gazelle, 2 SA-330 Puma, 3 Bell 206 L, 1 SA 315 Lama, 3 SA-318 Alouette II and 3 SA-319 Alouette III.

RCA: 1 AS-350 Ecureuil. CONGO: 1 AS-365 C Dauphin 2, 2 Mi-8 Hip. IVORY COAST: 4 AS-365 Dauphin 2, 3 SA-330 Puma. ERITREA:? Mi-8
ETHIOPIA: 1 SA-330 Puma, 10 Mi-6 Hook, 30 Mi-8 Hip, 30 Mi-24 Hind, 20 SA-316 and IAR-316 and Chetak
GABON: 5 SA-342 L Gazelle, 4 SA-330 Puma, 1 Bell 212
GHANA: 2 Bell 212, 4 SA 316 Alouette III.
GUINEA BISSAU: 1 Mi-8 Hip, 1 Alouette II and 2 SA-316B Alouette III.
GUINEA: 1 AS-350 Ecureuil, 1 SA-342 L Gazelle, 1 Mi-8 Hip, 1 IAR-316B Alouette III, 1 IAR-330 Puma.
KENYA: 1 SA-342 K Gazelle, 3 SA-330 G Puma, 26 Hughes 500 MD including 12 TOW, 9 IAR-330 Puma.
LESOTHO: 3 Bell 412, 2 MBB-105, 1 Bell 47G.
MADAGASCAR : 6 Mi-8 Hip. MALAWI: 6 AS-365 Dauphin 2, 2 AS-350 Ecureuil, 1 SA-330 Puma. MALI : 5 AS-350 Ecureuil, 1Mi-8 Hip. MOZAMBIQUE: 6 Mi-8 Hip, 4 Mi-24 Hind, 2 SA-316 Alouette III. NIGERIA: 2 AS-330 Puma, 12 AS-332 Super Puma, 26 MBB-BO-105
RWANDA: Several Gazelle and Alouette escaped from the civil war and found refuge in Zaïre.
SENEGAL : 2 SA-330 Puma, 1 SA-342 Gazelle, 2 SA-318 Alouette II.
SIERRA LEONE: 2 AS-355 Ecureuil, 2 Mi-24 Hind and 1 MBB-BO-105.
SOMALIA: (this stock is pre-civil war):1 AB-204, 4 Bell 212
SUDAN: 10 AB-212, 12 IAR-330 Puma, 20 BO-105, 6 Mi-8 Hip. TANZANIA : 4 AB-205B.
TOGO: 1 SA-330 Puma 1, AS-332 Super Puma, 2 SA 315 B Lama.
UGANDA : 2 AB-205, 2 AB-206, 2 AB-412, 2 Mi-8 Hip
ZAIRE : 1 SA-341 Gazelle, 9 SA-330 Puma, 1 AS-332 Super Puma, 6 SA-316.
ZAMBIA: 12 AB-47 G, 13 AB-205, 2 AB-212, 7 Mi-8 Hip.
ZIMBABWE: 6 AB-205, 9 AB-412, ? SA-316 Alouette III.

In Chad, RCA and Djibouti, France maintains DETALAT.
Here is a craft from DETALAT in Djibouti.

An Oryx from squadron 17 is about to lift a Jakal jeep of the 44th parachute brigade near Bloemfontein.

South Africa

Despite heavy budgetary restrictions the South African Air Force (SAAF), which has just celebrated its 75th anniversary, is one of the most effective in the continent. Following their combat experience in Angola and so as to overcome the international embargo, the S. Africans developed their own Super Puma, baptised Oryx and conceived the Rooivalk, an attack helicopter well-adapted to the bush.

Battle order:

Squadron 15: Puma/Oryx (Durban)
Squadron 17: Oryx (Swartkop Pretoria)
Squadron 19: Puma/Oryx (Louis Trichardt)
Squadron 22: Alouette III (Le Cap)
Squadron 87: Alouette III (Bloemfontein)
20 Rooivalk will be ordered and the MBB-117
of the old bantustans have been integrated into the SAAF.

Stock: 50 SA-330 Puma, 30 Atlas Oryx, 50 Alouette III

A test flight above the Kalahari for this Rooivalk.

An Alouette III and the famous Table mountain of the Cape.

CENTRAL AMERICA

Confronted with endemic guerrilla factions, most central American countries are equipped with Bell UH-1H and Cayuse serving as a reminder of the Vietnam war. The crews are generally well-qualified and the Salvador air force intensively carries out night flying. Cuba and Nicaragua reluctantly continue to use Russian material, a great quantity of which was delivered during the seventies and eighties.

El Salvador

Fuerza aérea de El Salvador

Hardened by a long struggle against Marxist guerrillas, the small Salvadoran air force is without doubt the best in Central America. There are three helicopter squadrons named: Escuadron Arce Acuna, Escuadron Monge Vides and Escuadron Cuellar Aguilar.

Stock: 10 Bell UH-1M, 40 Bell UH-1H, 14 Mc Donnell Douglas MD-Defender.

Mexico

Fuerza Aérea Mexicana.

6 SA-330 F Puma, 3 AS-332 Super Puma, 2 AS-355 F-2 Ecureuil, 15 Bell 212, 2 Bell 412, 2 Sikorsky S-70.

Guatemala

Fuerza aérea Guatemalteca.

The helicopters are regrouped within a squadron named *Ala Rotativa*. 4 Bell UH-1D/H Iroquois, 9 Bell 206 B/L, 6 Bell 212, 6 Bell 412, 3 Sikorsky S-76.

Cuba

Fuerza Aérea Revolucionaria.
36 Mi-8 Hip, 14 Mi-17 Hip, 12 Mi-24 Hind, 6 PZL Mi-2.

Panama

Servicio Aéreo Nacional.
5 UH-1H, 1 UH-1N, 3 Bell 212.

Costa Rica

This small and quiet country does not have an army as such but a Guardia Civil equipped with 3 Mc Donnell Douglas Hughes MD 500 E.

Honduras

Fuerza aérea Hondurren à L'escadrilla de Helicopteros which has about thirty craft is situated at San Pedro Sula at the Colonel Armando base.

Stock: 13 UH-1H, 9 Bell 412 SP, 3 Hughes 500 D and a Sikorsky S-76.

Dominican Republic

Two Aerospatiales AS-365 C Dauphin, 9 Bell 205 A 1 and a Hughes 500 serve in the Fuerza Aerea Dominicana.

Superb camouflage for this Bell-205 of the Dominican air force.

141

SOUTH AMERICA

Venezuela

The oil boom of the seventies meant that Venezuela could equip itself with a sizable aviation. Venezuela has, like all S. American countries, a guerrilla contingent but also a latent conflict going with Colombia. The air force has the 10th Special operations group equipped with helicopters but the majority are regrouped within the Aviacion del Ejercito Venezolano.

Battle order:

Air force: 10th Grupo Aéreo de Operaciones Especiales de Palo Negro with Squadron 101 on Bell-UH-1H, 212, and 412 and squadron 102 on Super Puma and Alouette III.
Army: 81st regimiento de Caballeria Aérea (812th and 817th Grupo).

Stock: 8 Agusta A-109, 16 Bell UH-1H, 3 Bell 205, 1 Bell 206, 8 AS-523 Cougar, 2 Bell 214, 2 Bell 412 SP, 10 SA 316 Alouette III.

Ecuador

The helicopters of the Fuerza Aérea Ecuatoriana are regrouped within the ALA de Combate 22 at the Simon Bolivar base at Guayaquil which has three helicopter squadrons (2211, 2212, 2213). Ecuador also has the 19th Brigada Aérea which has several helicopters. During the recent jungle war with Peru, these craft were used successfully without incurring any losses.

Stock: 6 Bell 206 B, 1 Bell-212, 5 SA-316 B Alouette III, 4 AS-350 B Ecureuil, 13 SA-342 K SA-342 L Gazelle, 5 SA-330 Puma, 6 SA-332 Super Puma, 1 Bell-214, 3 SA-315 Lama.

Colombia

Colombia has to use its helicopters against the drug cartels and also the Marxist guerrillas. Helicopters are attached to the CAATA (Comando Aéreo de Apoyo Tactico) belonging to Fuerza Aérea Colombiana. The CAATA includes escuadron 511 (Hughes 500), 512 (UH-60 A given by the Americans for the fight against drugs), 513 (UH-1H, UH-1B, AB-205, Bell 212), 514 (Bell 47 G). There is also a presidential flight on Bell 412.

Stock: 4 Bell 47 G, 22 Bell UH-1B/H, 12 Bell 205 A 1, 1 Bell 206, 5 Bell 212, 1 Bell 412, 5 Hughes 500 HM, 7 Hughes 500 MD Defender.

Brazil

This large country produces two types of helicopter under license using the Hélibras company, these are the HB-350/HB-355 F2 Esquilo (ecureuil) and the AS-565 AA Pantera (Panther). The air force or Força Aérea Brasiliera uses 6 SA-330 Puma, 7 AS-332 Super Puma and 37 Esquilo for transport and liaison.

Brazil also has an light army aviation whose HQ is at Taubaté and the main force is represented by the 1st Brigada de Aviaçao. This brigade includes the 1st Batalhao de Helicopteros and the Companhia de Helicopteros de Reconhecimento e Attaque on HA-1 Esquilos & Fennec and the Companhia de Helicopteros de Manobra on HM-1 Pantera.

Stock:
Exercito Brasileiro (Army) :
20 HA-1 (AS-550 Fennec), 36 HM-1 (AS-565 AAPanther),
16 HA-1 (HB-350 Esquilo).

Peru

The only country in South America to use Russian helicopters on a large scale, Peru has used them alongside Western machines against Maoist guerrillas and more recently in the border conflict with Ecuador. The air force and the army each have their own helicopter units.

Fuerza Aérea del Peru.
-3rd Grupo Aéreo: at Jorge Chàvez airport at Lima with 6 Escuadron de Helicopteros 311 on MI-24/35, Escuadron de Helicopteros 341 on MI-8/17, and four unidentified escuadrones on Bell-212, UH-1H, Bell 206 B, and BO-105.
-Grupo de Fuerzas Especiales Victor on MI-24 & MI-8.
"L'aviacion del Ejercito Peruano" operates with different types of helicopters mostly of Russian origin.

Stock: 12 Agusta A-109, 10 Bell-UH-1H, 11 Bell-206 b, 10 Bell 212, 5 Bell-214, 2 Bell 412, 24 BO-105C/L, 8 MI-6 "Hook", 70 MI-8/17 "HIP", 23 MI-24 "Hind", 7 SA-316 Alouette, 7 SA-315 Lama.

Guyana

The old British Guyana has one Bell-206 B Jet Ranger, one Bell-412 for VIP transport and two MIL MI-8.

Bolivia

Totally surrounded by mountains and situated at an altitude hardly favourable to the helicopter (except the small SA-315 Lama), Bolivia has nonetheless the 51st Grupo Aérea with 22 Bell UH-1H and 7 SA-315 Lama.

Paraguay

The helicopters of the Fuerza Aérea Paraguaya belong to the GAH or Grupo Aéreo de Helicopteros which has 2 Bell UH-1B, 3 Helibras HB-350 Esquilo and one MI-8 "Hip".

Chile

This long country with its "indefensible" borders, has without doubt the best armed forces in Latin America. The air force, or Fuerza Aérea de Chile, has in each one of its five brigades a small grupo bringing together some BO-105 for liaison, whereas the 9th and 10th grupo of the 2nd Brigada Aérea are composed of 17 UH-1 D/H used for light transport. The Comando de Aviacion del Ejercito de Chile has roughly thirty Puma and Super Puma transport helicopters and Mc Donnell Douglas MD-530 attack helicopters. The national firm of Cardoen is developing a light attack helicopter based on the Bell-206.

Stock: 17 Bell-UH-1D/H, 6 BO-105 CB,
1 MBB/Kawasaki BK-117, 17 SA-315 B Lama,
12 SA-330 F/L Puma, 3 AS 332 Super Puma, 5 MD 530F.

144

Argentina

A leading country in South America, Argentina possesses sizable armed forces but the military budget is affected by runaway inflation. The air force has several liaison helicopters but the majority is regrouped within the Comando de Aviacion del Ejercito Argentino.

Battle order:

Grupo de Helicopteros de Asalto 601
at Campo de Mayo Buenos Aires on UH-1H and Puma.
Grupo de Aviacion de Exploracion y Ataque 602
at Campo de Mayo, Buenos Aires on A-109.
8 Bell AH-1 Cobra are on order.
Seccion Aviacion N°6 at Neuquen on Lama.
Seccion Aviacion N°8 at Mendoza on Lama.
Seccion Aviacion N°9 Commodoro Riviera on UH-1H.
Seccion Aviacion N°11 at Rio Gallegos on UH-1H.

Stock: 31 Bell UH-1H, 8 Bell-212, 1 Bell-412 (on order),
6 Agusta A-109, 1 Sikorsky S-70 (VIP), 9 SA-315 Lama,
3 SA-330 L Puma, 3 AS-332 B Super Puma.
8 Bell AH-1 (on order).

Uruguay

This small country has in its air force or Fuerza Aérea Uruguaya du Grupo de Aviacion 5 some Iroquois and Bell 212.

Stock: 7 Bell UH-1 B/H and 2 Bell-212.

THE COMMONWEALTH

Canada

The helicopter makes a large contribution to the development of and the links within this enormous country. The Canadians build under license the majority of Bell models and play a major part in the manufacture of the model 412 HP Griffon which will replace the stock of medium helicopters of the Canadian army. It is the 10th Tactical Air Group which, apart from some SAR craft of the RCAF, regroup the helicopters of the Canadian Army.

Stock: 8 Bell CH-118 (UH-1H), 41 Bell CH-135 (UH-1N),
63 Bell CH-136 (OH-58 Kiowa),
14 Bell CH-139 (206 B Jet Ranger).
About a hundred CH-146 Griffon (Bell 412 HP) on order.

Battle order:

1st Wing Montreal: 401st and 438th squadron on CH-136.
2nd Wing Toronto: 400th and 411th squadron on CH-136.
11th Wing on different bases.
403rd squadron at Gagetown,
 New Brunswick on CH-135, CH-136 and CH-146.
408th squadron at Edmonton, Alberta on CH-135,
CH-136 and CH-146.
427th squadron at Petawawa, Ontario on CH-135 and CH-146.
430 squadron at Valcartier, Quebec on CH-136 and CH-146.
450th composite squadron at Ottawa on CH-135.

Australia

The Headquarters of the Australian Army Aviation Corps based at Oakey in Queensland governs the following units.
1st Division
1st Aviation regiment 161 squadron, Holsworthy on Bell 206B.
162 squadron, Townsville on Bell 206B, 171 squadron, Oakey on Bell 206B. 5th Aviation regiment with squadron A and B on S-70A and UH-1H based at Townsville. Training command at Oakey and Fairbairn on AS-350, UH-1H, AB-206 and S-70.

Stock: 18 AS-350 Ecureuil, 25 Bell-UH-1H, 43 Bell-206 B, 37 Sikorsky S-70 BlackHawk.

New Zealand

This country in the South Pacific zone has a squadron of Bell UH-1H within the Royal New Zealand Air Force. It is squadron N°3 based at Hobsonville. As well as its missions for the New Zealand army, squadron N°3 sends several machines to Auckland and Wigram for SAR missions.

The stock is composed of 14 Bell-UH-1H and 4 Bell 47 G for training purposes.

THE PILOTS

Leaving his sleeping bag, he has a brew and then wipes away the sand or dew that has gathered during the night on the cockpit of his machine. After a briefing, in a tent or a shelter, he and his crew go to the parking zone, which is sometimes within the reach of enemy fire. He wipes his feet very thoroughly so as not to cover the inside with mud. Next, the whistling of the turbines is heard, the rotor blades stir up the air, bending the vegetation or whipping up whirlwinds of dust… the rotors at full speed signal departure and, tipping its nose, the machine rises up. In the air, the muddy pilot becomes a god playing with gravity… but an extremely vulnerable god… who moves so very close to the ground to avoid the deadly impact which could so easily destroy his fragile machine. He carries out forward observation, he is an ambulance man, tank destroyer, a supplier of fuel or ammunition and a troop transporter. In the evening, before leaving on a night mission, he sweeps away the cartridge cases which are strewn across the cabin floor and occasionally will clean off the blood which is spattered on the seats… Far away from the large and cold air bases the helicopter pilot truly becomes the soldier of the sky.

THE FUTURE

In its fifty years of existence, the combat helicopter has definitively become part of the daily life of the combatant, and at the dawn of the 21st century a new generation of attack and assault helicopters is being born.

As is the case for combat aeroplanes however the sophistication of weapons systems, linked with economic difficulties and budgetary restrictions due to the fall of communism deeply affect the production of new models. In the area of light and reconnaissance helicopters, the very futuristic Boeing Sikorsky RAH-66 Comanche will possibly replace the Kiowa Jet Ranger.

Recent British and Dutch orders merely confirm that "you can't replace a winner" and that the AH-64D (also adopted by the US Army, which will modernise 760 AH-64 A to "D" standard) will, with the Eurocopter TIGER, be the attack craft of tomorrow. Digitalised piloting, firing control radar mounted on a mast connected to a ——————— coupled with a screen and a control system permitting this type of machine to localise 256 targets, to classify them (caterpillar track or wheels) and to select them before engaging the most dangerous.

Kamov-50 and Apache "Long Bow" will certainly dispute for their share of the attack helicopters' market. For transport, Sikorsky S-70 BlackHawk and Cougar will continue to criss- cross the skies for a long time yet, whereas the NH-90 of France, Germany, Italy and the Netherlands appears to be the assault helicopter of the next century. Its only current rival is possibly a land version of the EH-101 British Merlin.

Reliable and sure, due to their impressive airframes which are able to accept many modifications the CH-53 Chinook and MI-26 will certainly remain in service for many years. The combat helicopter of the future will be without doubt an ultra-sophisticated and stealthy machine, a hybrid of helicopter and airplane and perhaps even replacing the latter for low altitude missions. As opposed to the "robotized" jet pilot who receives his orders from an AWAC, the helicopter pilot, in spite of the sophistication of his machine, will have to use his own initiative and will doubtless keep alive the "fighter" spirit of the aviation of yesteryear.

Foreshadowing the "machines of tomorrow", the KAMOV 50 is both airplane and helicopter.

Solid and sophisticated, the Apache AH-64 D "Long Bow" is a worthy machine for the 21st century.

The NH-90, a European trump card, limited to the year 2000. It will replace the Puma, the latest Bell UH-1H and the BlackHawk.

Future master of the battlefield, the Franco-German Tiger will be a tank destroyer capable of breaking through enemy electronic defences.

Equipped with a "stealth" silhouette, the future armed scout of the US Army, the RAH-66 Commanche.

INDEX

ALOUETTE II

The Bundeswehr was the greatest military user with 226 SA-313Bs and 54 SA 318Cs put into service within the Heeresflieger-truppen from 1959. About fifty craft currently remain in service. In Europe, the light aviation of the Belgian ground forces has kept 20 Alouette II in both versions, whereas ALAT still uses machines essentially reserved for divisional Chiefs of Staff. Other military users are Benin, Cameroon, Central African Republic, Congo, Dominican Republic, Djibouti, Guinea Bissau, Ivory Coast, Lebanon, Morocco, Portugal, Senegal, Sweden, Switzerland, Togo, Tunisia and Turkey.

ALOUETTE III

South Africa, Angola, Austria, Burkina-Fasso, Burundi, Cameroon, Congo, Ecuador, Spain, France, Gabon, Ghana, Equatorial Guinea, Guinea-Bissau, Indonesia, Iraq, Ireland, Lebanon, Libya, Malawi, Mexico, Mozambique, Burma, Nicaragua, Pakistan, The Netherlands, Peru, Portugal, Rumania, Rwanda, Serbia, San Salvador, Switzerland, Surinam, Tunisia, U.A.E., Venezuela, Zaïre, Zimbabwe. The Chetak version is also in service in the Indies, Ethiopia, Nepal and the Seychelles.

OH-6 CAYUSE MD-500

Bahrain, Bolivia: 10 500Ms and 20 MD 530. Colombia: 20 500M and several MD-530. Costa Rica: 2 500M. Cyprus: 2 500s. Denmark: 12 500Ms. Salvador: 4 500Ms and 3 500s. Finland: 2 500Ds. Greece: 20 NH500s. Indonesia: 12 500s. Israel: 36 500MDs. Italy: 50 NH500s. Japan: 6 OH-6D, 164 OH-Ds and 65 OH-6Js. Jordan: 8 500Ds. Kenya: 2 500Ds, 15 500MDs, 15 500MD/Tow, 8 500Es and 8 500MGs. Mauritania: 5 500Ms. Mexico: 10 MD 520/530. North Korea: 66 500Es, 20 500Ds given by a German arms dealer. Philippines: 27 500MD and 28 MD530/520. South Korea: 509 MD/Tow of which 25 were built there and 144 500MDs. United States: 4 EH-6E, 16 MH-6E, 10 AH-6F, 16 MH-6H and 5 AH-6G used in the Special Forces.

AS-350 / AS-550

Abu-Dhabi, Australia, Benin, Botswana, Brazil, Central Africa, Denmark, Ecuador, France, Gabon, Guinea, Mali, Paraguay, Peru, Singapore, Tunisia. Algeria, Benin, Brazil, Djibouti, Fiji, France, Malawi, Sierra Leone.

BO-105

Bahrain (3), Brunei (6), Chile (6), Ciskei (1), Colombia (2), Dubai (6), Germany (304), Spain (68), Indonesia (30), Iraq (75), Jordan (3), Kenya (1), Lesotho (2), Netherlands (28), Peru (24), Sierra Leone (3), Sweden (20), Trinidad & Tobago (1).

GAZELLE SA-341 / 342

Abu-Dhabi (11), Angola (13), Burundi (2), Cameroon (4), Cyprus (12), Ecuador (13), Egypt (96), France (340), Gabon (5), Guinea (1), Iraq (40), Ireland (2), Jordan (2), Kenya (1), Kuwait (20), Lebanon (7), Morocco (24), Qatar (14), United Kingdom (216), Rwanda (6), Serbia (319?), Slovenia (1), Syria (55), Trinidad & Tobago (2), Tunisia (2).

206-JET / OH-58 A/B/C

Italy: 150 AB-206 C1. Austria: 12 AB-206 A 1. Saudi Arabia: 20 AB-206A. Morocco: 20 AB-206 A/B. Sweden: 19 AB-206A known locally as Hkp 6A. Iran: 80 AB 206A/B. Greece: 17 AB 206A. Libya: 5 AB-206A. Malta: 1 AB-206A. Oman: 3 AB-206B. Sharjah: 3 AB-206B. Slovenia: 2. Spain: 4 AB-206A. Tanzania: 2 AB-206B. Uganda: 4 AB-206A (police). Yemen: 6 AB-206A/B.

AS-365

Angola: 16. Brazil: 36. China: ?

SIKORSKY S-76 / H-76

Chile: 1 S-76 VIP. Korea: 150 H-76 produced under license. Dubai: 1 S-76B. Spain: 8 S-76C. Guatamala: 4 S-76B. Honduras: 1 VIP. Jordan: 18 S-76 B. Iraq: 2 S-76B. Philippines: 17 AUH-76 of which 12 are armed with 12.7 Herstal HMP-0.50 pods.

AH-1 F / S COBRA

USA: 800 models of which 42 are TAH-1S for training. Argentina: 8 on order for 602 squadron. Israel: officially 30 AH-1F, but there are certainly more. Japan: 88 AH-1F of which 70 constructed under license. Jordan: 24 AH-1F. Pakistan: 30 AH-1F. South Korea: 42 AH-1F plus 28 on option. Rumania: 96 AH-1F on order for 1999. Thailand: 4 AH-1F. Turkey: AH-1S/F.

MIL MI-24 HIND

Afghanistan: 60 Mi-24 A,D,E. Algeria: 30 Mi-24 A,D,E. Angola: about 30 Mi-24 E and F. Armenia: 13 Mi-24. Azerbaidjan: 10 Mi-24. Bulgaria: 45 Mi-24. Byelorussia: 80 Mi-24. Croatia: about 12 Mi-24 certainly ex-Ukrainian. Cuba: 12 Mi-24. Czech Republic: 20 Mi-24 D and 20 Mi-24Vs. Ethiopia: about 12 Mi-24 certainly non-operational. Germany: 50 Mi-24 D and Vs from ex E. Germany. Hungary: 22 Mi-24 D and 8 Mi-24Vs. India: 25 Mi-24D plus thirty Mi-35 Hind E. Iraq: 40 Mi-24 D,E,F. Kazakhstan: number unknown. North Korea: 50 Mi-24s. Kurghistan: number unknown. Laos: 8 Mi-25 unconfirmed. Libya: 26 Mi-24 A,D,E. Mozambique: 15 Mi-24. Nicaragua: 6 Mi-25S. Pakistan: a certain number of machines delivered by deserters. Peru: 24 Mi-25. Poland: 29 Mi-24 D and Vs. Russia: ? Sierra Leone: 4. Slovakia: 19 Mi-24 D and Vs. Syria: 50 Mi-24. United States: several examples. Ukraine: 270 Mi-24. Vietnam: number unknown.

W-3 SOKOL

Bulgaria (14), Czech Republic and Slovakia (38), Cuba (2), Djibouti (3), Hungary (31), Iraq (number unknown), Lesotho (2), Libya (number unknown), Nicaragua (2), South Korea (number unknown), Poland (113), Rumania (6), CIS (750), Syria (20), Germany (44 withdrawn from service).

AH-64 A/B APACHE

United States: 813, Egypt: 24 + 12 on order, Greece: 12 on order + 8 on option, Israel: 42, Netherlands: 36 on order, Saudi Arabia: 12, United Arab Emirates: 20 + 10 on order, United Kingdom: 67 on order.

UH-1H

Austria: 24 AB-204 of which 8 remain in service. Germany: 352 UH-1D. Saudi Arabia: AB-205. Argentina: UH-1 D & H. Australia: UH-1H. Bahrain: AB-205 A. Bangladesh: AB-205A. Bolivia: UH-1H. Brazil: UH-1 D & H. Brunei: AB-205 A. Canada: UH-1H. South Korea: UH-1B & H. Dominican Republic: AB-205. Dubai: AB-205 A. El Salvador: UH-1H. Spain: UH-1C & H. Greece: UH-1H and AB-205. Guatamala: UH-1H. Honduras: UH-1H. Iran: AB-205 A. Italy: 120 AB-205. Jamaica: AB-205 A. Japan: UH-1B and H. Mexico: AB-205 A and UH-1H. Morocco: AB-205A. Burma/Myamar: UH-1H. New Zealand: UH-1H. Oman: AB-205. Pakistan: UH-1H. Panama: UH-1B & H. Peru: AB-205A. Philippines: UH-1H. Singapore: UH-1B and H. Sweden: AB-204. Taiwan: 118 UH-1H. Tanzania: AB-205. Thailand: UH-1A,B & H. Tunisia: AB-205.Turkey: 180 AB-205 and 40 UH-1H. Uruguay: UH-1B & H. USA: 2500 UH-1 A & B, 2008 UH-1D, 3573 UH-1H. UAE: AB-205. Venezuela: UH-1D. Yemen: AB-204. Zambia: AB-205. Zimbabwe: AB-205.

BELL 212 / UH-1N ET AB-212

Argentina. Saudi Arabia: 30 AB-212. Austria: 24 AB-212. Bangladesh. Brunei: AB-212. Canada: 50 CH-135. Chile: AB-212. South Korea: AB-212. Dubai: 1 AB-212. Ecuador: AB-212. Spain: 6 AB-212. Ghana: AB-212. Greece: AB-212. Guatamala: AB-212. Guyana: AB-212. Italy: 40 AB-212. Iran: AB-212. Israel: AB-212. Japan: AB-212. Lebanon: 7 AB-212. Libya: AB-212. Malta: 2 AB-212. Mexico: AB-212. Morocco: 7 AB-212. Panama: UH-1N & AB-212. Philippines: UH-1N. Dominican Republic: AB-212. Salvador: B-212. Sudan: 11 AB-212. Sri-Lanka: 12 AB-212. USAF: 79. USMC: 221. Thailand: AB-212. Tunisia: UH-1N. Turkey: AB-212. Yemen: 6 AB-212. Zambia: 2 AB-212.

BELL 412 ET AB-412

Bahrain, Botswana, Canada, Colombia, South Korea, Dubai: 3. Guatamala, Guyana, Honduras, Indonesia, Italy: 30 plus some extra orders. Lesotho: 2. Norway, Peru, Slovenia: 7. Sri lanka, Thailand, Uganda, Venezuela: 2. Zimbabwe: 12.

EUROPCOTER SA-330

Abu-Dhabi: 9. South Africa: 65. Argentina: 1. Cameroon: 2. Chile: 15. Ecuador: 1. Spain: 5. Ethiopia: 1. France: 155. Gabon: 4. Guinea: 1. Indonesia: 14. Iraq: 22. Kuwait: 6. Lebanon: 9. Malawi: 1. Morocco: 3. Nepal: 2. Nigeria: 2. Pakistan: 35. Portugal: 10. Rumania: IAR-330 (90). United Kingdom: HC. Mk 1 (41). Senegambia: 2. Togo: 1. Zaire: 9.

EUROPCOTER AS-532 COUGAR

Abu-Dhabi: 8. Argentina: 24. Brazil: 10. Cameroon: 11. Chile: 2. China: 6. South Korea: 1. Ecuador: 6. Spain: 29. France: 30. Gabon: 1. Indonesia: 7. Japan: 3. Jordan: 12. Malaysia: 5. Mexico: 4. Nepal: 1. Nigeria: 2. Oman: 2. Panama: 2. Netherlands, Qatar: 12. Singapore: 28. Sweden: 12. Switzerland: 15. Togo: 1. Turkey: 30 (plus 30 on order). Venezuela: 18. Zaire: 1.

SIKORSKY S-65 / CH-53

Germany: 110. Israel: officially 45 but certain information leads us to believe that the number is greater as the Yas'ur programme involves 64 modernisation kits.

MIL MI-26 HALO

India: 10 examples in squadron 126 at Chandigarh CIS and Ukraine.

MI-8 / 17 HIP-C ET HIP-C

Afghanistan: Mi8 and Mi-17. Algeria: 12 Mi-8 plus ? Mi-17. Angola: 40 Mi-8 and 18 Mi-17. Armenia: ? Bangladesh: 5 Mi-8 and 5 Mi-17. Byelorussia: ? Bosnia: at least 7 Mi-8. Bhoutan: 2 Mi-8. Bulgaria: 7 Mi-8 and 19 Mi-17. Cambodia: 7. China: 30 Mi-8. Congo: 2 Mi-8. North Korea: 70 Mi-8/Mi-17. Croatia: 15 ? Cuba: 20 Mi-8 and 16 Mi-17. Egypt: 50 Mi-8 out of 120 delivered. Ethiopia: 35 Mi-8 delivered. Finland: 7 Mi-8. Germany: the Mi-8 of ex E. Germany were withdrawn from service in 1995. Guniea Bissau: ? Guyana: ? India: 140 Mi-8 and Mi-17. Iraq: 100 Mi-8. Kazakhstan: ? Laos: 9 Mi-8. Libya: ? Mi-8 of which 1 Mi-9 and 2 Mi-17 P EW. India: 140 Mi-8 and Mi-17. Iraq: 100 Mi-8. Kazakhstan: ? Laos: 9 Mi-8. Libya: ? Mi-8 of which 1 Mi-9 and 2 Mi-17 P EW. Macedonia: 3 Mi-8. Madagascar: 2 Mi-8. Mali: 1 Mi-8. Moldavia: ? Mi-8. Mongolia: 12 Mi-8. Mozambique: 6 out of 15 Mi-8 delivered. Nicaragua: 10 Mi-8 TBK and 15 Mi-17. Uzbekistan: ? Pakistan: 10 Mi-8. Paraguay: 3 Mi-8. Peru: 51 Mi-8 and 27 Mi-17 some of which were recently lost in combat. Poland: 50 Mi-8/1. Rumania: 25 Mi-8/17. Russia: ? Slovakia: 9 Mi-8 and 19 Mi-17 plus 1 Mi-8 PPA. Sudan: 4 out of 8 Mi-8 delivered. Syria: 100 Mi-8/17. Tadjikistan: 10 Mi-8. Turkmenistan: ? Czech Republic: 32 Mi-8 and 31 Mi-17 plus 1 Mi-9 and 2 Mi-8 PPAs. Ukraine: ? USA: several Mi-8/17 serve in evaluation units of the US Army. Vietnam: 50 Mi-8/17. Yemen: 55 Mi-8/17. Yugoslavia: 50 Mi-8. Zambia: 7 Mi-8.

SIKORSKY S-70 A / UH-60

Saudi Arabia: 13 S-70 A-1 Desert Hawk and 8 S-70 A-1L medevac. Australia: 39 S-70 A9 manufactured under license. Bahrain: 1 UH-60 A and 2 UH-60 L. Brunei: 2 S-70 A. Colombia: 10 UH-60 A. China: 24 S-70 C-2 (officially civilian). South Korea: 100 of local production of which 19 UH-60 P delivered by Sikorsky. Egypt: 2 S-70 A. Hong Kong: 2 S-70 A. Israel: 10 UH-60 (certainly more but the figures are held secret). Japan: 21 UH-60 J. Mexico: 2 S-70 A. Morocco: 2 S-70 A. Taiwan: 14 S-70 C. Turkey: 12 SA-70 A. United States: 1400 UH-60 A/L, 66 EH 60 C electronic war, 98 HH/NH - 60 SAR and specia operations, 22 MH-60 K on order for special operations.

MIL MI-6 HOOK

Algeria, Angola, CIS, Egypt, Ethiopia (withdrawn from service), Iraq, Indonesia (withdrawn from service), Laos, Pakistan (withdrawn from service), Peru, Poland (withdrawn from service), Syria, Vietnam (withdrawn from service), Ukraine, Zambia.

The author would like to thank all those pilots, officers, NCOs who helped him with this book, also Mr Peter Steinemann, a great name in aerial photography and Alain Fournier who opened their archives so as to find "the rare bird". A big thankyou to "Mickey" who helped me enormously in the search for illustrations.
The photos belong to the author with the exception of the following:
FOURNIER Archives: p 25 (top), p 79, p 83 (centre right), p 85 (top), p 88 (bottom), p 107 (centre), p 107 (bottom), p 115 (centre), p 115 (bottom), p 134 (top), p 141 (centre).
Peter STEINEMANN: p 15 (top), p 17 (bottom), p 19 (top), p 33 (bottom), p 48 (top), p 79 (top), p 83 (top left), p 83 (top right), p 85 (bottom), p 102 (top), p 105 (bottom), p 112 (top),p 116 (top), p 116 (bottom), p 117 (bottom), p 127 (bottom), p 128, p 129 (top), p 129 (bottom), p 130 (top), p 130 (bottom), p 135 (top), p 135 (centre), p 139 (bottom), p 140 (centre), p 140 (bottom), p 142 (top), p 143 (top), p 146 (bottom), p 147 (centre). Eric MICHELETTI: p 33 (top), p 134 (bottom), p 135.

Paolo VALPOLINI: p 10 (top), p 54, p 56 (bottom) p 107 (top), p 127 (bottom).
Frédéric LERT: p 11 (top), p 17 (top), p 19 (bottom), p 72 (bottom), p 83 (centre left), p 137 (top), p 138 (bottom), p 139 (top), p 150 (top).
Gille RIVET: p 40, p 82 (bottom right), p 93 (top), p 93 (bottom), p 131 (top), p 143 (centre), p 143 (bottom).
Antonio ES CARMO: p 141.
DEFENSA: p 14, p 140 (top), p 141 (bottom), p 142 (top), p 143 (top).
AIR WORLD JAPAN: p 83 (centre), p 122, p 132 (top centre, bottom), p 133.
Ishihara DTM TAIWAN: p 83, p 133.
EUROCOPTER: p 32 Claude Leclerc, p 74.
Bernard Lehn: p 113, p 151.
AUSTRALIAN AIR FORCE: p 122.
MC DONNEL DOUGLAS HELICOPTER: p 150.
SIKORSKY: p151.
ATLAS AVIATION: p 75 (top and bottom), p 137.
Thierry CHARLIER: p 100.
ECPA: p 37, p 117.
TASS: p 59, p 72 (top), p 108 (top), p 109 (centre).